SPLASH!

'A witty and revealing story of life on newspapers,' is the verdict on this book by Charles Orr who describes in entertaining style a colourful panorama of comedy and drama — from early days on a country weekly to the stormy 'revolution' that ended Fleet Street, the traditional Street of Adventure.

The author, who has worked on leading newspapers, news and feature agencies in Ireland, Britain and overseas, has met many famous personalities — and some of the remarkable events narrated have the excitement of a 'whodunnit'. His gallery of people and incidents, ranging from the remarkable R.M. Smyllie of the *Irish Times* to the international 'media giant' Rupert Murdoch is huge. His story amuses, diverts and informs.

The book covers a remarkable variety of events and experiences — including censorship secrets, scandals, kidnappings, murder mysteries — while working with such organizations as the *Irish Times*, *Daily Mail*, Press Association, Reuters, *Sunday Dispatch*, *News of the World* and other papers. Recalling 'nasty situations' in which he has been involved the author says attacks by dogs were the worst. Once, bitten on the face, he had his wounds bathed in a nearby pub with whisky. He and his wife Dorothy, an accomplished musician, have two sons and two daughters.

SPLASH!

DRAMA AND COMEDY IN A
NEWSPAPERMAN'S CAREER

Charles Orr

MERLIN BOOKS LTD.
Braunton   Devon

For
Dorothy
Carol and Trilby
Charles and Patrick
and my Mother

*Past deeds still travel with us from afar
And what we have been makes us what we are*
George Eliot

ISBN 0 86303 423-3
Printed in England by Antony Rowe Ltd., Chippenham, Wilts

FOREWORD

Charles Orr is a splendid storyteller. He parades in front of us not only his fellow newspaper folk, among whom he has spent his life, but other personalities famous and obscure: Charles Chaplin, Sean Bourke, accomplice of the spy George Blake, the Lennons — John, Cynthia and Yoko Ono — and many others who at various times made news. Some appear in short vignettes, others with more detail, but all shift briskly across the stage; there are no *longueurs*. Charles presses on to the next anecdote, the next change of scene, the next profile.

We do not hear too much about Charles himself. As a good reporter, he chooses to remain so often in the background. And all journalists are reporters.

He was on the *Irish Times* when Smyllie, Myles na Gopaleen, Paddy Campbell (later Lord Glenavy) were in their prime. This phase of his career he evokes with particular verve.

There are characters whom he does not name. One of them, referred to as The Senator (which he was not), could be worthy of a novella.

I read this book straight through, non-stop. It also lends itself to being taken in piecemeal. It deserves to be read by all those who practise that old Black Art we call the daily press and by anyone who enjoys a good story.

Douglas Gageby
former Editor, the *Irish Times*.

CONTENTS

ILLUSTRATIONS

ACKNOWLEDGEMENTS

The contents of this book are based on my own experiences while working for newspapers and agencies in Britain, Ireland and overseas, but I acknowledge the valuable assistance of Mr Ken Gray, Deputy Editor *Irish Times,* and Mr John Gibson, Chief Librarian, Mr Kenneth Withers, former Editor *Belfast News-Letter,* the staffs of the National Library, Dublin, and Linenhall Library, Belfast, Mr Phil Wrack and many other journalist colleagues.

The following books and official papers were among the sources consulted:

The Secret Army: J. Bowyer Bell
The Second World War: Sir Winston Churchill
Dail Debates 1939-45: Dail Eireann
The Newspaper Book: Hugh Oram
As He Saw It: Ralph ('Bud') Bossence
The Devil You Know: Jack White
My Life and Easy Times: Patrick Campbell
Dublin Opinion 1939-45
Patrick Kavanagh: the Complete Poems: Edited by Peter Kavanagh
Strained Relations: T. Ryle Dwyer
Editing and Design: Harold Evans
The Newspaper, an International History: Anthony Smith
Spies in Ireland: Enno Stephan
Ireland in the War Years: Joseph T. Carroll
Dublin From Downing Street: Sir John Peck
A Man Called Intrepid: William Stevenson
The End of the Street: Linda Melvern
The Life and Death of the Press Barons: Piers Brendon
An Irishman's Diary: Patrick Campbell
Oliver St. John Gogarty: Ulick O'Connor
In Time of War: Robert Fisk
Hold Your Hour and Have Another: Brendan Behan
Cruiskeen Lawn: Myles na Gopaleen (*Irish Times*)

States of Ireland: Conor Cruise O'Brien
Modern Newspaper Practice: F. W. Hodgson
The Emergency: Irish Times Supplement: ed. Ken Gray
Unneutral Neutral Eire: R. M. Smyllie
Ireland's Stand: Eamon de Valera
Dangerous Estate: Francis Williams
The Strategy of Confrontation: Official Chicago Report.
Across the Narrow Sea: Sam Hanna Bell
The Journalist's London: Philip Gibbs
The West Britons: Brian Inglis
Changing with Changing Times: Irish Times Supplement: Tony Gray
The Best of Myles: edited by Kevin O'Nolan
News Group Newspapers — For kind permission to reproduce certain photographs and quotations while interviewing Charlie Chaplin, Archbishop Lefebvre, Sean Bourke, the former Cynthia Lennon, Mayor Daley of Chicago, Pope John Paul and others while engaged on many news and feature stories.
Irish Times — For kind permission to reproduce photographs of R. M. Smyllie and Alec Newman, and other matter, including certain quotations of Myles na Gopaleen.
Associated Newspapers — For kind permission to reproduce photographs of the Duke of Westminster, Princess Margaret and Lord Snowdon and quotations concerning the second Earl of Iveagh, Sir Compton Mackenzie and others — including persons associated with notorious murder cases.

Chapter 1

FOLLOW THAT ROWING-BOAT!

"Sorry — I couldn't help laughing" Charlie Chaplin

Charlie Chaplin emerged stealthily from the side door of the hotel, an absurd figure in a long raincoat reaching down almost to his ankles. An old felt hat was pulled down over large dark glasses. The famous comedian was on holiday with his wife Oona and family at Waterville, an angling resort in County Kerry, and I recognized him in that disguise only because I was chasing him for a story and interview.

So far no pressman had succeeded in talking to him. "He's touchy when on holiday and talks to scarcely anyone outside his family," I had been warned. Chaplin, who spent a good deal of his time on Lough Currane trying to catch his first trout, had twice given me the slip. He ignored notes sent to him, but I still haunted his hotel where he had a suite of rooms.

One day after he had lunched I noticed his chauffeur-driven limousine waiting in the hotel courtyard — but no sign of Charlie. Then the car moved off. I went to the rear of the hotel. In a few moments Oona and three of their children came out by a back door and entered the car. Again it moved off but stopped after a short distance. Still no sign of the star.

Then from the side door emerged this strange figure in the flapping raincoat and ridiculous hat — Charlie, like some character out of one of his old films! I couldn't help but burst out laughing at his disguise. He stopped and then grinned, too, at the absurdity of the situation. But when I moved forward he jumped nimbly into the car which drove off at speed towards Derrynane sands.

Gone picnicking, it seemed. But there was no trace of him or the family on the sands, or at nearby Ballinskelligs where they sometimes went sand-yachting. "We'll try the lough. He may have doubled back," I told my photographer colleague Harry MacMonagle, from Killarney. At the lough we spotted a few small boats out by Church Island. From a tiny jetty we got a closer look. Sure enough, there they were, Charlie in the stern of their craft fishing for that trout.

The problem was he might land anywhere along the lough shore. So

11

— there was this rowing-boat moored at the jetty — and looking very lonely. "Come on," I said.

"Hope you can row," Harry grinned.

It was a long, choppy pull out towards the island. A couple of figures back at the jetty were waving vigorously. "Friendly chaps," said Harry.

As we drew close the ghillie in Chaplin's boat waved to me to keep clear of Charlie's line streaming astern, and the actor wagged his head in mock disbelief at the two bobbing figures in pursuit, one photographing, the other questioning. Oona didn't look too pleased, but the children Josephine and Victoria, then in their early teens, and 10-year-old Eugene were enjoying my efforts to keep our boat in position and Harry's endeavours to avoid going over the side with his camera.

At length the ghillie turned for the shore and the Chaplins were moving away from the jetty as we reached our mooring place. But they stopped to watch as they became aware of our hot reception from the two figures we had seen waving — a purple-faced gentleman and his boatman. They had had a good morning's fishing and were eager to get back on the lough — hence the purple hue. "Who gave you the right to take this boat?" roared the gent, his fists clenching and unclenching.

Apologies, explanations — "Very sorry . . . emergency . . . had to contact Mr Chaplin . . . glad to compensate . . . " Unhappily one's feet becoming entangled with Purple's Face's fishing gear did nothing to help the situation. And I could see Chaplin's shoulders shaking and the three children giggling. Then Chaplin raised outstretched hands in a brief gesture of conciliation. Purple Face and the boatman, still simmering, loaded up their outraged craft and pulled away, to my relief.

Chaplin, now affable, said: "Sorry, I couldn't help laughing at that little scene — an embarrassing moment for you." Perhaps he saw in the incident an idea he might have used in one of his famous comedies of earlier years.

Meeting Charlie Chaplin face to face like that was an unforgettable experience — the magical genius whose artistry and antics had held millions throughout the world spellbound over the years. And here he was, smiling at me! I at once was aware of what can only be described as a sense of 'power' emanating from him. He had strong compelling features, his eyes were brilliant and his gaze seemed to go through you. The comic actor in him took over and as the camera clicked he made a mock display with the small fish he had caught. "I'm going to have this chap for my breakfast," he said. During our talk he told me about many of the subjects in his autobiography, which was published some time later.

Chapter 2

THE DOG THAT STOPPED
A WEDDING

*And the reporter who thought
he was the 'Cisco Kid*

That Charlie Chaplin adventure was well removed in time and circumstance from my first introduction to newspaper life — as office-boy and general dogsbody on a small weekly country newspaper.

"Hope you can make a decent drinkable cup of tea," was the grouchy greeting. The Editor, who was also a farmer, used to clump around the office in not too hygienic wellington boots. The few reporters there had their own tea-mugs with their initials crayoned on the enamel. I found this depressing — surely they should have been swigging liquor neat from a bottle. I must have been watching too many films.

One day, after a few months, the Editor came into the room suddenly and found me reading *The Times*. This must have been a severe shock to him. Nobody in that Ulster office ever read any national newspapers, to my knowledge.

"I'm giving you a trial as a junior reporter," he told me a few days later. Then: "You could hardly turn out much worse than the other layabouts round here." I thought: should I tell him my real reason for reading *The Times* that day — to see what they said about the England-Ireland Rugby match at Lansdowne Road? No — let him think whatever he liked. He was the Editor.

It was a weird office. Even I saw that there was no proper control. How the paper came out each week was a mystery. An elderly dame kept the accounts — so-called — on bits of paper in boxes, desks and in cupboards. Each Friday when paid (ha!) I had to sign a slip of paper which she sometimes put in her handbag.

When nobody was looking — so she thought — she took an occasional gulp of whiskey from a bottle in her locked desk. Once when she caught my glance she smiled and said: "Doctor's orders — have to keep the wheels lubricated."

That Friday pay-packet, though small, was still appreciated by my mother who at the time was keeping boarders because my father had

13

died while I was quite young. The circumstances of his death after becoming involved in a historic political incident are mentioned in a later chapter. My mother had earlier been almost broken by the death of my four-year-old only sister Ethel, whom she adored — but she rose above these blows with wonderful courage and spirit.

The boarders she looked after in fact unconsciously helped her survive and overcome that tragic period of her life — especially the antics of John, a young hospital doctor whose amorous adventures kept the rest of us intrigued. Although by no means the tall, dark, and handsome type John was nevertheless pursued by the girls who loved his infectious gaiety and personality. Some even called at the house and he advised us all: "Tell them I'm out, or on holiday, or I'm dead, or anything you like to get rid of them."

My mother used to say, "It's a mercy he hasn't the looks of a film star — then we'd have no peace at all."

Then he got involved with a Channel swimmer, a foreign girl called Mercedes Gleitz. She was attempting to swim from Donaghadee, Co. Down, to Portpatrick in Scotland — a tough challenge. John went along as the doctor in the boat crew which accompanied her in case of accident.

As it happened a severe storm suddenly blew up and the waves in the North Channel — a notorious area anyway — became so violent that the girl had to be hauled out of the sea and the swim attempt abandoned. Conditions worsened and the party, driven many miles off course, eventually had to land on the remote island of Ailsa Craig to take shelter. They were marooned on the small rocky spot in the Firth of Clyde for a couple of nights.

When he eventually got back John told us about the ordeal — "Those lighthouse men saved us," he said. But he seemed very reluctant to talk about Mercedes. "Oh, I just treated her for a few jellyfish bites. She's gone off to Germany," he remarked. But next day he received a letter and exclaimed, "Good heavens, she's going to call here. Tell her I've left, I've gone to Australia — anything."

Once when there was a knock at the front door he hid in the alcove under the stairs. Then we told him, "You can come out now, it was only the milkman." Eventually Mercedes left for the Continent and John breathed again.

"She must have got over those jellyfish bites," said one of the boarders with a wicked grin. "We'll never know now just what happened on that island."

The boarders were quite an assortment. They included a 'double act' who stayed occasionally when they were touring theatres and concert halls. The man was a juggler and wire-walker and his wife an acrobatic dancer. They were very good. The odd thing was they scarcely ever spoke to each other. The only words the man ever uttered were addressed to his dummies — he practised ventriloquism in their bedroom. It was strange that the two, who could 'bring the house down' with their stage act, should seem so distant with each other. Then they ceased visiting us and we wondered about them. Later we heard that the man had died after a road accident — and his wife died later from an overdose of drugs.

"Like a couple of swans on a lake," said my mother afterwards, "seemingly ignoring each other, yet remaining side by side and pining if they're apart."

Then there was a young woman teacher who sang and played the piano — off-key sadly in both cases. And a salesman who at weekends got drunk and played the flute. One evening he arrived at the house followed, like a Pied Piper, by a horde of kids all singing lustily to his flute version of The South Down Militia:

You've heard of Julius Caesar and great Napoleon too
And other famous hairymen that fought at Waterloo
But if you've read your history you'll quickly understand
The South Down Militia is the terror of the land.

My favourite among our guests was a Miss MacKissock, an independent lady, sister of a professor. Although very old she was young in heart, elegant and graceful in manner, knowledgeable and humorous. She seemed interested in everything. Sometimes during our chats she would assume outrage over some newspaper story. Looking agonizedly heavenwards she would exclaim, "Oh you terrible journalist people!" — her good-natured mockery and banter were a delight.

She liked company and yet she also seemed quite happy to be alone. I wondered about this and she once told me, "Happiness is within you. What matters is the way one thinks — to have resources within one's self."

On another occasion I happened to mention someone who had remarked, "The days of miracles have passed." She smiled, shook her head and exclaimed, "How can anyone say such a thing? Miracles are everywhere — all around us and in us."

A remarkable lady. Not one to become involved in anything vulgar, squalid or down to earth nastiness. Yet one day we were astounded to learn that she was to appear in court.

"Can't believe it," exclaimed my mother. "Must be some mistake."

But she did appear in court — as a witness against a man accused of beating up a boy in a park. The court heard that she had encountered the incident when out walking and glancing from time to time into her favourite novel Jane Austen's *Emma*. Without hesitating she immediately seized the man — considerably larger than herself — and marched him along to the police station. The court expressed its admiration of her intervention to save the boy and the man was put on probation.

Scout camping and Rugby were among my keenest interests then and my closest pal was Rex Galloway — so close that we unselfishly loved the same girl! Emily, a redhead. His first love, mine too. At 16 or so Rex and I never even thought of jealousy. Once while camping beside Lake Windermere we even 'went halfers' and sent her a box of chocolates. After we got back home Emily said, "The chocolates were squashed in the post."

Later Rex, ever faithful, said, "I should have wrapped the box more carefully."

I, not being so devoted, said, "She never said thanks." Rex glanced at me, shocked. Dear Rex. Some years later he joined the Royal Air Force — and in the RAF he died. I have never met any finer person since.

But back to my time on that country weekly paper . . .

One day when passing a local church I noticed all the signs of a wedding about to take place — cars with white ribbons, guests all togged out in their best. But suddenly the bride-to-be rushed out of the church to her car followed by agitated relatives and friends. In tears she was driven away quickly. She had been 'stood up' by her fiancé after a last-minute row over, of all things, her pet spaniel. She wanted to take the dog along with them on their honeymoon. He said No. What began as a love-me-love-my-dog tiff blew up into a bitter quarrel with hard words, and the bridegroom was unrelenting.

Good story for our paper, I thought — a change from dreary council reports. But back at the office nobody was interested. The girl was the daughter of a business man advertiser and they wouldn't use a line. It seemed such a waste — so, on to the phone to the chief reporter of a daily newspaper in Belfast — John Parker, of the *Northern Whig*, and Peter

Robinson, the *Daily Mail's* staff man. They lapped up every detail — ages, colour of the girl's hair and eyes, the name of the dog and so on. The story got a good show in the two papers the next day with pictures and I felt ten feet tall — but back in our own office nobody mentioned it. Later — a couple of cheques in the post. What riches! But the best reward of all, thanks to John Parker, followed in a few months — a move to the 'big city' — Belfast — as a staff reporter on the *Northern Whig*, owned by a wealthy family, the Cunninghams, stockbrokers with industrial interests. The boss 'Big Jimmy', Master of a famous pack, made a tall and memorable figure when occasionally he stalked through the office in full hunting gear. He contributed the 'Hunting Notes' usually referring to 'our deer' in his descriptions of the day's sport. 'Our deer' always seemed to escape in fine style.

* *

"We haven't got elastic columns. You can't get a quart into a pint pot"
> — Old Shaw's rebuke to wordy reporters.

* *

The Editor, who was also a well-known politician, used to keep a revolver in the top drawer of his desk. During his frequent absences the leading articles were written by his deputy, a worried man who seldom spoke to anyone. When his proofs required correcting he shuffled into the sub's room, muttered something to Old Shaw, the Chief Sub-editor, and retreated. He never ventured into the composing room, fearing to confront Norton, the fiery overseer who ran the place like the swashbuckling captain of a pirate ship.

Copy from the subs' room was shoved through what was known as the 'box' into the composing room. It had a sliding pull-down door and one of Norton's pastimes was to bang it down suddenly thereby 'guillotining' the hand of the unwary. The sub most able to get the better of Norton was Sammy Goldstein who yelled: "I've told the Rabbi about you. He's coming round to circumcise you, you old sod."

One night I had to take a story I had written to the deputy editor, who was doing a leader on the subject of the story. I expected to find him at his desk with his customary morose look. But his chair was vacant. Then I saw him half-lying on the big couch near the window, watching me. I approached and held the copy out to him. He made no reply when I spoke. His eyes stared fixedly up at me. It's the first time he has ever really looked at me, I thought. "This is the copy you wanted," I repeated. But there was no answer, no movement, just the continuing stare.

I rushed out to Old Shaw and said: "We'd better phone for an ambulance right away." The ambulance men carried the deputy editor down the stairs, not on a stretcher but in the chair he had so often used when writing his leaders. He died shortly afterwards.

Some of the staffmen on the paper later made names for themselves — Roy Suffern, who became an executive of the Mirror Group; Robert Lynn, a subsequent MP and knight; Leonard MacNae, an editor on the Press Association and author of a standard work on newspaper libel law; Owen Senior, of the National Union of Journalists; Kenneth Withers, Editor of the *News-Letter*, a rival daily paper; William Armour, an Editor who, though eventually dismissed, made local history in a tussle with the Establishment; Philip Blake, an author on specialized subjects; Bruce Proudfoot, Robert Beattie, Jimmy Sherrard, Jack McGladdery and Jack Atkinson, all of whom, along with the Rosenfield sisters, Ray and Judith, achieved distinction in their profession.

But there was one who achieved the wrong kind of distinction and who was responsible for some of the strange happenings in that office — as on the day when suddenly there was a deafening bang and a shower of glass splinters poured over my notebook and desk while, about my head, the metal lamp shade, now minus its electric bulb, swung wildly.

Across the reporters' room Miley gazed along the barrel of his air-pistol as he lined me up. He was chewing a wad of gum and for the moment I was his Wild West target. Then he lowered the weapon and grinned; "You got off that time, laddie, on account of I'm gonna let you buy me a pint."

Miley and his gun were the talk of the office where he had arrived a few weeks earlier sporting a red and yellow check shirt, corduroy pants and — a sombrero. He had been engaged through the London office who had made no mention of the Wild West connection. On his arrival at our office he got a cool reception from his new chief John Parker, a hard man, who muttered, "Bloody hell," glanced at his watch, and made for the door saying, "I'll be in my office if you need me" — which being interpreted meant he would be in the Half Moon bar across the street.

As a reporter Miley was efficient but unorthodox. Stories which other staffers would take a column or more to cover he might dispose of in ten paragraphs. Old Shaw declared gloomily, "That bloody man is going to land us right in it one of these days, mark my words." White-haired, red-faced, thin as a rake, the chief sub was seldom referred to by his first name John. Nobody knew Old Shaw's age. Subs and reporters who'd been in the office for years said, "He was just the same when I first came here." Always ready for a set-to with anyone, his white moustache would bristle at the approach of one or other of his enemies such as Norton and certain proof-readers. And now he had Miley whose off-hand way of addressing him as "Old Timer" set him fuming. "Impudent ass," he growled.

But it was Miley's behaviour during off-duty hours which caused greatest comment. He had been spotted on a bicycle careering around suburban streets in his cowboy get-up with a lariat swinging from a shoulder. Every so often he would take his hands off the handlebars and lasso some astonished old lady or other passer-by. Then his big grin: "Guess I'd better set you free now, pardner."

At a press conference he got into a row after referring to a well-known local actor as 'a pansy'. The office buzzed with the stories. "Bit of an eccentric — I'll have a word with him," said Parker.

"Eccentric? That fellow should be put away," declared Old Shaw.

Miley approached me one day: "Laddie, you should get yourself some insurance." I replied that I couldn't afford the premiums. He snorted, "Hell with premiums. I mean get yourself a shooter."

It was that shooter of his which proved Miley's undoing. In the reporters' room one evening I took a call from the receptionist in the downstairs 'front office' — "Is Miley there? Two gents down here would like a word."

The tone made me ask cautiously: "What do they look like — the law?"

"You said it," was the reply.

"Miley — couple of chaps in the front office want to see you."

He looked up — "Peelers?"

"Sounds like it."

Miley leapt to his feet, grabbed his coat, and made for the door. Before vanishing he turned and called to me: "Thanks, laddie. Look after yourself. Don't forget what I told you about insurance. Adios."

He shot down the back stairs to the street, and was never seen again in the city. It was learned that earlier that day he had become involved in an argument in the Half Moon and had seen off somebody's pint with his shooter. He was spotted boarding the night boat for Liverpool.

Chapter 3

THE GIRL ON THE SHIP

"Never answer any questions that you're not asked!" Stewarty Black

"The office won't be the same without Miley," said my pal George who was typing out a police court story. This was some tribute coming from George whose escapades kept the office smiling. His father, a country rector, had been requested to remove him from boarding-school because of 'unruly conduct'. The last straw, it was said, was the temporary disappearance of a housemaster's new motor cycle. George was a motor-bike enthusiast. He now had an old Norton of his own and I had a Scott Squirrel two-stroke. We had been friends since our first school-days.

Now as we tinkered with our bikes we often set the world to rights; about girls, God, the universe, and the social system.

One day after we had made a hasty escape from a crowd during a riot in the upper Falls district — we had foolishly started photographing some gentlemen sniping with revolvers at cemetery gates and had got away on George's Norton — he said: "I suppose you don't believe in miracles, you iconoclast?"

"Well, it was a miracle we got away on that old heap you call a motor bike. How about you?"

"I think everything's a miracle — I think the universe is the greatest miracle. If nobody ever saw any stars in the heavens and suddenly one night the stars all filled the sky can you imagine the sensation? People would go mad." George was keen on the stars, could point out constellations and tell you all about them.

There was something else that George was keen on. Her name was Marjorie. She worked in a down-town shop and the two were together at every opportunity. "She keeps telling me how terrific life would be if we were married," he said "but I'm afraid she'll have to wait awhile."

George and Marjorie — talk about uninhibited! When those two were together the windows became clouded. She came to George's digs once while I was there.

"What do you want me to wear tonight, darling?" she asked after they had unclinched.

20

"Your black nightie," replied George promptly. "And Marje — I've got a list of other things you're to wear."

"Goody, George — what things?"

"Transparent stockings with sexy designs for a start."

"Haven't got stockings like that."

"You will have tonight, kiddo."

"What else, pet?"

"Suspender-belt, a little red number — can't wait to see you in it, Marje."

"Red for danger, George you devil."

The two were on the couch now and they didn't notice my departure.

But a few weeks later it became obvious that something had gone wrong, and they were no longer seen around together. Then one morning George told me briefly: "Marje is seeing another bloke."

A few evenings after that, looking shaken, he said: "I want you to come with me and try to find her — she's gone."

He had discovered that she had taken up with a ship's officer. This man's vessel was laid up in port, the crew was dispersed, and he was living on the ship as officer of the watch, so to speak. George believed that Marje was with him and he declared: "Maybe she's being held there against her will."

At the docks a harbour police officer stopped us. We explained we were reporters inquiring about a missing woman. It was pitch dark when we found the ship, huge and silent, tied up at a wharf. We ascended a gangway and as we boarded the vessel our footsteps sounded loud against wood and metal. We climbed up and down steps and felt our way along passages. At one point George narrowly avoided stumbling about 20 feet on to a dimly-lit metal-plated deck below.

Was the ship deserted I wondered? But some minutes later we came upon a cabin where a light was showing. Still no sound. We hammered on the door — silence — then after a minute or so the door was opened. There standing before us were Marje and a man, hand in hand.

"We've come to get you away from this place," said George. His voice sounded strange.

Marje, very cool, said: "You needn't have bothered coming here, George. There's nothing now between you and me. There never was much. I'm married now. I'm staying on this ship. We got wed this morning — see?"

She raised her left hand showing a wedding ring. George, too stunned to speak, just stared. The other man stepped forward, reached out and the two shook hands. Then Marje said: "Well, goodbye, George." The two went back into their cabin and closed the door.

"Let's get away from this," muttered George.

Back on the quayside we set off, with no word spoken, towards the Half Moon. We drank automatically. I had never known him to remain silent for so long. After a few pints he said: "We seemed so close. She wanted me to marry her. She said so. How could she marry somebody else? So quickly? Almost a stranger. How could she do that?"

We got fairly drunk that night without finding any answer.

Another shock was in store for George. A few weeks later he was fired — a victim of one of those economy waves. But he never moaned about it. "Never mind. I'll get by OK," he said with a smile.

The funny thing was he did — thanks mainly to a betting system he invented. Always keen on horse-racing he now spent hours each day in the sitting-room of his digs surrounded by race record books and the daily sports pages. He filled notebooks with figures and calculations based on runners' breeding and form, weights and placings, distances and state of the going. He studied jockeys' records, horses for courses — everything except their horoscopes.

He devised a graduated table of points awarded under each heading and placed his bets accordingly. But sometimes he would flout his own system and back the second or third rather than the runner with most points — "Must allow for chance you know." And luck was often on his side. Some weeks he found himself with more money than when he had been working. He never once failed to pay his weekly rent. His old landlady, who fussed over him as if he were her own son, kept telling him: "You mustn't work so hard, love." She never realized that he had lost his job. Neither did his folks back home at the rectory.

By present standards wages then, the thirties, sound farcical. Some journalists, expected to be always on call, were getting only £3 or £4 a week. Some, myself included, made extra cash by acting as correspondents for British and other newspapers.

But if wages were low so were prices and we 'lived it up' with golfing trips, dinner dances, theatres, weekend jaunts. We dressed up in 'tails' for the Grand Central Hotel or the Slieve Donard or a hunt ball 'down the country'. Often the cost for the evening, including the drink, could be kept under ten quid! One could see a double feature film programme AND a variety show for 18 pence or two shillings.

Early one morning as George and I and two girls were returning from a dance at Islandmagee, Kitty, George's new friend, demanded to be allowed to drive. It was my first car, an eight h.p. Ford and desperately expensive, I thought, at £100 new. A tank-full of petrol cost just under ten shillings.

"I'm a great driver," Kitty assured us. She started off with discord of gears which caused some anguish. Then we began hurtling along with a deviant abandon, and anguish changed to alarm. "Ah, sure it's these heels," chortled Kitty. "There's not enough room under the pedals for my high heels."

George said, "Oh,well, if that's all we needn't worry."

Then it happened — Kitty took a bend in the road at speed and the car veered across a grassy patch and hit a cottage, the bumper against the front door.

"Sorry," said Kitty, but she was giggling as she moved out of the driving-seat. The cottage door opened and the sleepy householder mumbled, "Were you knocking?" More giggles from Kitty.

Then the man, suddenly wide awake, began kicking up a shindy about the damage to his door. I apologized: "Just a slight mishap. Terribly sorry. Will pay for the repairs — no need to inform the police."

He retorted, "No need at all — I happen to be a police officer." Stunned silence. I thought Ah, Love! Could thou and I with Fate conspire . . . I had visions of a court room, the angry magistrate — "Drivers like this must be taught a sharp lesson" — a big fine, maybe a licence suspension.

To my vast relief the man relented and said, "Don't let it happen again!" Thankfully he had a sense of humour. In the end, with further apologies on my part and the handing over of a fiver, all was forgiven — and we were invited in for a cup of tea!

The Half Moon, our nearest pub, was also the haunt of a droll character on the staff — Stuart Black, or 'Stewarty' as he was always called. He couldn't write ordinary shorthand — yet he could turn out virtually verbatim reports, where necessary, of City Council and similar meetings. His own peculiar system was allied to a sharp memory. Quite a comedian himself he was never seen to smile but councillors and court staffs loved his deadpan wisecracks and some officials would talk to him where they would say "No comment" to other newsmen. On occasion he actually joined in discussions at some council meetings without objections. It was generally understood that he had another part-time job — in an undertaker's, for which his expression of extreme melancholy must have been ideal.

He loved practical jokes. Once after a huge traffic jam built up around the city centre the culprit responsible turned out to be Stewarty. Masquerading as corporation officials he and a couple of cronies armed with tapes leisurely measured from pavement to pavement while queues of cars piled up and the streets resounded with the hooters of angry drivers. And late at night there would be a phone call to the reporters' room: "Hello." — pause — "Is that yourself?" — pause — "Have you heard the news?" — pause — "The old squire has been found, foully murdered." — pause — "Make sure to put me down for a credit. Ta, ta." Then you would know Stewarty was in good form round at the Nightworkers' Club. Actually it was his way of 'keeping in touch.' When there was a big story and a lot of work to be done there was no better fellow than Stewarty.

And he could dispense his own brand of wisdom at times — his repeated advice to younger colleagues was: "Never answer any questions that you're not asked."

One Christmas Eve night Stewarty, George and I having celebrated the occasion decided to go and see Jimmy O'Dea in panto at the Empire Theatre. The comedian was a great favourite with Belfast audiences and the famous old theatre, now gone, was packed for the second house. We three had to stand at the back of the stalls along with many others. Standing stolidly just in front of us were three men in the audience wearing hard hats — which tickled us greatly for some reason. They kept telling us to be quiet — so, suddenly on impulse, we each grabbed a hard hat and raced down the centre aisle pursued by three angry men.

On the stage at that moment a comic and his dog were in the middle of their act. They both stopped abruptly and stared at our onrush. Stewarty neatly skimmed the hat he had seized towards the stage and the dog leapt to try and catch it. The audience roared appreciation. George and I planted our purloined hats on the grinning heads of two trombone players in the orchestra pit. The conductor flailed at us with his baton.

We three fugitives fled in different directions, Stewarty through an Exit to the right, and George and I to the left. George made for a flight of stairs. I found myself near the Gents so darted in and locked myself in a cubicle. Nothing for it but to wait for a while. But I dozed off and on waking all was silent and pitch black. The theatre was closed and I was locked in. It's a strange experience feeling one's way around in a dark, silent, deserted theatre — eerie. I managed to get out eventually, through a window.

Said Stewarty sternly later: "I trust that you two fully realize that what you did that night was entirely irresponsible and uncalled for."

"Yes, Stewarty," we said humbly.

Chapter 4

'A SOLDIER'S FAREWELL'

"The Editor's leading article will get us all fired"
John Parker, Chief Reporter

The thirties was a time of intensified newspaper warfare among the big national dailies. The circulation battle of the 'Press lords' Rothermere, Beaverbrook, Kemsley and Camrose took on amazing forms. Readers were cajoled with big insurance offers and with prizes of all kinds — a country pub, cars, houses, luxury holidays abroad with thousands of pounds spending money. News scoops were in demand as part of the campaigns and Old Shaw often phoned 'late' copy to the *Daily Mail's* Manchester office.

One evening when phoning over a story abut a Government dinner party at Hillsborough Castle he referred to a married couple among the guests "the Bishop of — and Mrs — ." The telephone line was poor and the copy-taker in Manchester was unable to get the wife's name properly, so Old Shaw shouted "And Mrs repeat Mrs — mistress." He was using the last word in its old sense meaning mistress of the household, the wife, in his efforts to make the copy-taker understand. He was perspiring after it all.

About fifteen minutes later the Manchester office phoned back. "That you, Shaw. I say, there could be a good story for us in that piece you've just phoned — the bishop and his girl-friend. Old devil, eh — how long has this been going on?"

"How do you mean, bishop and his girl friend?" Old Shaw bristled.

"Come on, the bishop and his mistress at the Castle dinner party. I've got the copy here before me — could be a good yarn, what?"

As light began to dawn Old Shaw gasped, "Bloody fool on the phone."

Then he went on "No, no. I wasn't talking to you. There's no story about a bishop and his mistress. Somebody got the wrong end of the stick" — and he explained what had happened on the phone earlier. The conversation went on for a few minutes longer, Old Shaw kicking his legs out behind him and his face turning deeper red with fury. Then he slammed down the receiver exclaiming, "Cheeky young bounder — he should go and teach his grandma how to suck eggs."

His curious habit of kicking his legs out behind him while leaning, hands on desk and talking had an unfortunate consequence one night — unfortunate, that is, for Sammy Goldstein who incautiously ventured behind him while the old man was telling me about a hair-raising coach trip he had experienced in Sardinia. Sammy encountered a shattering left foot just where it wasn't required. He turned a greenish colour and tottered towards the gents.

Often when holding forth about Mozart, or Alekhine's best chess game, or the most enjoyable way to travel from Venice to Athens, Old Shaw seemed young as a lad — mimicking and playing the part of some character he had encountered. He had known Lord Northcliffe and liked to relate how he had changed the whole style of journalism and built up an 'empire' of newspapers.

"Once during the troubles," he said, "all communcations were cut off and we couldn't get any stories across to London or Manchester. I got a great exclusive story with the help of Peter Robinson and got my wife to take it over to the London office by boat and train. It made a big splash. They were delighted. I got a fat fee, the Editor in London took my wife out to lunch, and his secretary bought her a new hat as a present."

Said George one day in the Half Moon: "Old Shaw seems to know everything, to have been everywhere and to remember everything. He told last night about Ward-Price of the *Daily Mail* once putting on his expenses sheet £5,000 for buying a ship in the Far East when he was chasing a story."

George, although no longer on the staff, often wandered into the office to look up racing details in the files, and with the hope of maybe getting his job back.

I agreed with him about the old boy and declared: "Old Shaw is timeless, evergreen, imperishable, immortal. He first came into prominence in Palaeolithic days about half a million years ago when he began showing primitive man how to fashion stone implements. Thousands of years later he was instructing their descendants in the use of fire for cooking."

George interrupted: "Look, they're about to take the last orders."

"When Christopher Columbus was facing disaster his old shipmate John Shaw was there at hand to rally the crew and so discover the New World. And who do you think was the real discoverer of the art of printing? Need you ask? And Wellington would never have . . . "

But George had dashed over to order a couple of pints.

Dear Old Shaw — wise, funny, understanding, tolerant and

intolerant, aged yet youthful and ageless, wonderful — immortal! I heard some years later that he had died. Strange how such ridiculous stories start up! "They told me, Heraclitus, they told me you were dead . . . " But I know better.

There was a doubly dramatic incident a few evenings later in the same hostelry as a group of us listened to the radio broadcast by Edward the Eighth announcing his abdication because, he said, he could not continue as King without the support of "the woman I love."

In the dead silence which followed his final words on that occasion, "God save the King," there was a muffled half-sob from one of our colleagues as, in tears, he turned away and left hastily. None of us made any comment but each one of us was acutely aware of his personal problem and the strain that he was under, particularly at that moment. In a way he, too, was faced with an abdication of a somewhat different sort — a break with his family because of a contemplated 'mixed marriage'.

The family made strenuous efforts to dissuade him and to prevent any wedding. It was a trying and emotional situation — the sort many parents dreaded — but despite being torn in feelings and affections the two young people did marry and, overcoming difficulties, succeeded eventually in making a happy future for themselves and their children.

* *

"I sing best after a few bottles of stout — say, about a dozen"
— the late 'Bud' Bossence, one of
Belfast's most popular newspapermen.

* *

The most sensational event on the paper occurred during the editorship of William Armour, who associated himself actively with public affairs as no other Editor had done. We heard one night the tramp of an army of feet on the stairs. "It's the IRA going to take over the paper," exclaimed Sammy Goldstein jumping to his feet and grabbing his typewriter. But the tramping feet turned out to be those of a huge delegation of farmers invited in by the Editor for consultation.

Armour, son of the celebrated 'Armour of Ballymoney' and, like him, liberal in outlook, sought improved pay and conditions for staff and actually threatened to resign if these were not granted. In the event he did not resign, he was fired! Not because of his demands but because he offended the Establishment with his biting criticisms of official policies. Matters came to a head when he attacked plans for the new Craigavon Bridge at Derry.

On his last night at the office he wrote a blistering leader headed 'A Soldier's Farewell'. It created a tremendous sensation proferring a two-fingered gesture in print 'Goodbye and . . . . you' to Establishment and management alike. There was crisis atmosphere next day and evening in the office. Parker and Shaw were sent for and hauled over the coals. How had they allowed the leader to slip through? Why hadn't they drawn attention to its contents? Production of the paper was held up as the two desperately tried to defend themselves. Reporters and subs gathered in groups and there were rumours that the paper was to shut down.

When the couple eventually emerged Old Shaw exclaimed, "My job's on the bloody line. I don't know yet whether I'm fired or not."

Said Parker: "That leading article will get us all fired. They can all go to hell." He spent the rest of the night in the Half Moon.

Neither man was dismissed. The editorial staff held a meeting to protest over Armour's sacking. But nothing came of it and a new Editor Frank Adams, from Staffordshire, was appointed.

* * *

Some occasions, after a time, go down in local history or folklore, and so it was with the Great Office Party organized in honour of Big Jimmy's engagement, to a lovely heiress. All contributed to a wedding gift presented at a Saturday night dinner in a city hotel, and a musical programme was arranged. But many of the guests and artistes had started celebrating earlier at the Half Moon and the Duke of York's. The 'Duke's' in Commerical Court, also a haunt of newspapermen, was frequented by such as Ralph (Bud) Bossence, a great humorist still remembered with affection (he died in 1971), Jimmy Kennedy, Jimmy Boyd, Cecil Orr (no relation), James Kelly and 'Hammy' McDowell.

Because of the preliminary celebrations the Office Party got off to a shaky start — and I mean shaky. When John Parker came on for a duet with Jean Murdoch, "Oh, no John, no John, no," he swayed, reached out for the piano, missed it and then lurched against it. Jean supported him, literally, amid a string of interruptions. The front office manager, known as 'be Jasus' because of his initials B.J., tried to make an impression with 'Drink to me only with thine eyes' — but this prompted Billy Stanley, a thirsty reporter, to make for the door shouting, "Anyone coming for a pint?"

But worse was to come. A sub-editor who should have known better began reciting 'The Bells'. The room exploded in uproar all providing their own version and the audience were in hysterics. The speeches did nothing to aid the party and a sub-editor Alec Riddell who unwisely wound up with, "There's nothing on God's earth to equal the love of a good woman," was assailed with cries of "I wouldn't say that" and "Wheel him out."

Big Jimmy, shaking with laughter, seemed to enjoy the proceedings. His fiancée, looking uncertain, must have wondered how this lot ever managed to produce a daily newspaper.

Meanwhile a personal problem loomed at this stage — lack of sleep. Working many late nights, then rising early to attend lectures at Queen's University eventually became a burden, threatening one's Rugby, golf and tennis activities! Also, Armour, a tireless man himself, had recruited me to run weekly classes for prisoners at Crumlin Road Gaol. Some gifted characters there — one chap surprised me by producing an almost perfect reproduction of my newspaper which he had done with pen and ink — he was a convicted forger.

Many mornings, still half-asleep, I cantered into the university area by the back gates, past the medical school where some wags had painted 'BRAINS' on a large box at an upper window. "Late again, late again," they chanted on seeing me. I yelled back, "Pick a few out of that box for yourselves."

I soon learned there how to yawn without opening my mouth, especially during the lectures of one professor — a chap with a shaggy black beard and a repulsive red shirt. He was, all agreed, incomprehensible and one morning, unable to take any more, we all burst into roars of laughter. He exclaimed, "If any gentleman would like to leave the room . . . " But we were already tramping out, hooting. Again, during an exchange, he demanded, "You — your name?" from a student. The chap answered "Hill." The professor cried, "Can't you even pronounce your own name? It consists of four letters pronounced Heel." But Hill to his eternal credit raised a roar of laughter by replying in tones audible to those around him, "And your name consists of four letters pronounced Sheet."

After two years it had to be Goodbye, Queen's, I love you, but one just has to get some sleep.

And, in any case, a change in career was just around the corner . . .

Chapter 5

SMYLLIE'S PEOPLE

The Palace Bar 'set' and the alligators

A note arrived for me from R.M. Smyllie, the celebrated Editor of the *Irish Times* — widely respected then, as now, as the country's most influential newspaper. I had met him previously through a relative of mine and, like other journalists, was well aware of his often abrupt and whimsical style. His note read: *Dear Orr — Morrison Milne will be in Belfast on Tuesday next and I'd like you to meet him in the Grand Central Hotel at lunch-time. After you've had a chat come and see me in Dublin. P.S. — Milne wears plus-fours.*

Smyllie at the time was planning further changes in the lay-out and content of his paper which had only recently begun putting news on its front page. Milne, an Aberdonian still retaining a splendid Scottish accent after many years in Dublin, introduced himself as Chief Sub-editor. He explained that the paper was "Under scrutiny because of its old-fashioned appearance," and Smyllie was anxious to give it a more attractive look and content without upsetting its more conservative readers. From what they had heard, he said, they believed that I could help in this and he offered me the job of deputy chief sub-editor with this specific duty.

A meeting with Smyllie was arranged for the following week. Apart from resulting in my moving to the *Irish Times* it was for me an outstanding and memorable occasion — lunch with the great man at Jammet's, the famous old restaurant, now gone of course. And later with new colleagues, Kevin Collins, Alec Newman & Co., a Joycean pub tour — Mulligan's, Davy Byrne's, the Brazen Head, Brian Boru, the Bailey . . .

Robert Maire Smyllie, a legendary figure even in his own lifetime, was a Falstaffian character — by turns humorous and taciturn, charming and rude, logical and yet unpredictable. To a man of his temperament — at heart pro-British and Unionist, one who despite being in the public eye was really a loner and, as it emerged, hated having to make decisions — his position as Editor then was arduous.

At a time of changing circumstances one sensed that he perhaps made things even more difficult for himself through a seeming inability to take anyone fully into his confidence. At our meeting, for example, he merely said that things on the paper, "Need improving and brightening up — you know what's wanted." He waved further discussion aside with, "Oh, Milne has explained all about it."

What he did chat about was the Arnott family, owners of the paper, and Major Lawrence Knox, who started it up in 1859 — "Fought in the British Army during the Crimean War, you know." Smyllie himself had taken over the editorial chair from an autocratic John Healy who during his pre-war regime ignored virtually everyone and dined only with the proprietor, then the second Sir John Arnott.

To the *Irish Times* staff at Westmoreland Street — where the main entrance was then situated — Smyllie was 'R.M.' and, only to fairly close friends, 'Bertie'. He inhabited a small untidy office with a glass roof — an unworthy setting, it seemed, for any Editor. It contained an old bulging roll-top desk into which he crammed things which he couldn't be bothered reading. One night when his desk was covered he swept everything, including a number of unopened letters, into his big waste-paper basket. I said, "Excuse me, you've thrown away a lot of unread letters I believe." He blew a cloud of pipe smoke and laughed, "Never mind, if there's anything important they'll write again."

He shared his office with his deputy Alec Newman, a former Classical scholar and teacher who spoke rather in the Malcolm Muggeridge style. The two, so different in personality, got along well together in a bantering manner with polite exchanges of erudite insults and innuendoes. Both excellent linguists their leaders usually contained Classical quotations. Newman was a linguist in another sense and when he had had a few too many he could fairly turn the air blue — an attribute which years later cost him dear.

Despite their abilities and years in the job neither man had much practical knowledge of or deep interest in the production of the paper and seldom ventured into other departments. It was an inherited situation, and while the news-gathering side was excellent the same could not be said of the *laissez-faire* sub-editorial department. The make-up of pages was left to the composing-room 'stone men'. After all, things had been like that for generations and it wasn't until 1941 — the year Germany invaded Russia and Hess landed in the United Kingdom on a 'peace mission' — that news stories were carried regularly on the front page. There had been one exception — a special Sunday edition was produced in September 1939 with a front page story of the German invasion of Poland.

As Editor, Smyllie divided much of his leisure time between the nearby Palace Bar and the now-vanished Pearl Bar. The Palace was his favourite. Settled happily with his pipe going he attracted Dublin's so-called literary set and an assortment of hangers-on. Amused by the gossip and behind-backs tales he listened more than he talked. These groups often included writers and artists such as Brinsley MacNamara, Patrick Campbell, Austin Clarke, Seumas O'Sullivan, Donagh MacDonagh, Frank McManus, William Conor, Harry Kernoff, Cathal O'Shannon and, of course, Brian O'Nolan alias Flann O'Brien alias Myles na Gopaleen.

Smyllie enjoyed the farcical personality clashes which occurred from time to time in the Palace lounge and which bewildered visiting writers and critics in search of reputed 'wit and brilliant conversation'. The hopes of these visitors were realized when in the company of such as Sean O'Faolain, but some unwary strangers — especially those with obsessions about the writings of James Joyce — found themselves at times verbally ambushed by resident controversialists. Cyril Connolly, literary editor of the *Observer*, once called the pub, "A cultural excrescence," but singled out Smyllie and Seamus O'Sullivan, Gogarty's friend, as its outstanding personalities. And he went on, "The Palace is as warm and friendly as an alligator tank."

The Editor commented, "He's right — but there are alligator tanks everywhere. Newspapermen have to watch out. The human alligators are always waiting to rush and destroy them." He may not then have fully appreciated the relevance of his own words. If he had remembered them, and if he had been stronger, things might have been better for him later.

Silent or otherwise in the pub Smyllie dominated merely by his presence. But he could be testy and capricious, suddenly slamming down his glass and marching out of the bar without a word if somebody or something offended him — as I observed one evening after he had a curt exchange with the poet and writer Patrick Kavanagh whom he usually tried to avoid.

To escape people waiting to button-hole him he used different entrances to the office and varied his arrival times. Often he avoided them by slipping round the corner, dodging the cavalry charges of bicycles then in car-less Dublin, and entering the building through the dispatch department. When he couldn't prevent a confrontation he used his 17-stone bulk to charge through the group grunting, "Not now, very busy, some other time."

*   *   *

"Good-evening Mr Smyllie sir," was Alec Newman's invariable greeting when R.M. arrived in the office. One night I heard him add, "Those fellows up at the Castle cut a lot of our stuff to hell last night." He was referring to the wartime Censorship officials to whom proofs of leading articles, news, features and headlines had to be submitted at the Dublin Castle offices.

Smyllie grunted, "It's time I had another word with those gentlemen." Then he added, "In the meantime Mr Newman, tonight you will do a war situation leader dwelling on the significance of the HMS *Hood* episode and the supply position — and Mr Newman . . . "

"Sir."

"Kindly try not to be so bloody obscure this time."

"With great respect Mr Smyllie sir — bollocks."

Then R.M. remarked with a malicious grin, "Your bucolic friend Kavanagh was lurking in the vicinity this afternoon. You might suggest to him that he should remain with his own cronies at McDaid's." (Kavanagh was from County Monaghan and his genius had not yet been appreciated or recognized.)

Newman retorted, "Sir, as you well know, I have no bucolic friends. Alcoholic, yes, even at times paralytic — but bucolic, no. May God preserve us from all these smelly culchies who would take over the Elysian haunts of our fair city."

Pleased with these preliminiaries Smyllie burst into song:

> *"What news of princes, dukes and earls.*
> *Pimps, sharpers, bawds and opera girls?"*

Occasionally he would chant parts of his leading articles when revising — or warble a 'soupçon of Mozart' as he described it.

Later at night, having completed their articles, Smyllie's custom was to start on his brandy bottle, and Newman on his Power's Gold Label whiskey. R.M. was the better drinker, always coherent and in control. Alec when he became elated could be caustic to proof-readers or others who might approach with an inquiry.

Despite their banter then and the bright lights of Dublin it was a critical period of the war and the Editor had this in mind when he mentioned the famous HMS *Hood*, which had just been sunk by the

German battleship *Bismarck* — he feared it could affect the future course of the war. In the event the *Bismarck* herself was soon crippled and sunk by the British after a long-running battle.

As they sat there drinking Smyllie and Newman never dreamt that only a few nights later they would hear German bombs crashing on the nearby North Strand area of Dublin killing 29 people. Many of the victims, including children, died in the blazing rubble, but reporters' stories were heavily censored and some of the photographers' harrowing pictures were never published.

Alec Newman, Deputy to the celebrated R. M. Smyllie whom he succeeded as Editor of the Irish Times — *but the exuberant and outspoken Newman later had to resign.*
(*Photo:* Irish Times)

W. S. 'Willie' Armour, controversial Editor of the Northern Whig, *Belfast. After his dismissal he wrote a fiery leading article headed 'A Soldier's Farewell' which caused a furore.*

Chapter 6

THE GINGER MEN

"We mustn't turn the Old Lady into a scarlet woman"

Smyllie and Newman, even after some lapse of time, never seemed really happy with news appearing on the front page! Certainly Newman didn't take to the change — "we're like pimps living off the earnings of press prostitution," he declared. Alec had a nasty habit of 'killing' headlines or 'intros' when the Editor's proofs were delivered. If he saw, say, a single-column story with a three-column heading he exclaimed, "Bollocks," and slashed his green-ink pen across the headline not comprehending, or caring, that the story was intended to 'treble up' underneath it. The same thing happened regularly with other proofs resulting in delays and savage words at make-up time on the 'stone'. (What a contrast to today's more efficient and cleaner techniques!)

This period coincided with the appearance at the office of a so-called 'ginger group' of shareholders. Their arrival in fact, not realized at the time, marked the beginning of the end of control by the Arnott family. Heading the group was Frank Lowe, a Dublin business man who later became chairman. Smyllie, accustomed to the personal confidence and friendship of the traditional owners, was unhappy with the turn of events — "Blow-ins and bloody grocers are trying to take over and run the paper," he growled.

The group organized 'editorial conferences' to discuss aspects and content of the paper. R.M. attended these with some reluctance. He made no attempt to conceal his frigid attitude but sat in aloof and disdainful silence surrounded by his close colleagues. Also attending the 'conferences' was the foreman of the composing-room, a testy old boy who regarded the conferences with contempt and made audible disparaging comments. R.M.'s massive shoulders shook from time to time and although his expression did not change I figured that the Editor was laughing inside!

At one conference a ginger group spokesman pinned up that morning's page one and began questioning its content — headlines, the 'splash' story, various 'intros' and the lay-out. When Smyllie and Newman made their comments in reply and referred to the attractive appearance of the page the spokesman declared: "We mustn't keep concentrating on such matters as appearance and headlines . . . the *Irish Times* is the Old Lady of Westmoreland Street, a blue stocking. We must not make her into a scarlet woman offensive to readers."

This at last jolted the Editor. He heaved himself up suddenly in his chair and said abruptly: "I think the page looks well. The lay-out is good and, from what I hear, readers are pleased with the improved appearance of the paper. I intend to continue on the way we are now going."

It was a real broadside, coming from R.M., and the rest of us felt like applauding. "Bravo" exclaimed Newman and he stood up saying, "Class dismissed, I take it."

The 'editorial conferences' were quietly dropped soon after that — but R.M.'s relations with the newcomers were uneasy. He detested being 'organized'. Once when office routine was discussed, and it was suggested he should make himself available at specific times for appointments and such, he affected not to hear, turned to his gregarious colleague and friend 'Pussy' O'Mahony and the two, chatting and laughing, sauntered off to the Palace Bar.

The *Irish Times* was not making much profit then. Competition was keen especially from the rival *Irish Independent*, and the *Irish Press*, founded in 1931 — 'de Valera's paper' as it was often called — was also pushing hard under Editor Bill Sweetman and news editor Jack Grealish. Smyllie, despite all the problems, did much to carry his paper through arduous years. Later, after he had ceased to be Editor, the continuing effects of his work contributed to the paper's post-war growth and eventual prosperity.

* * *

In between his encounters with management on the one hand and censorship officials on the other Smyllie loved to chat with his colleagues and friends* — the late Patrick Campbell, who brought a gifted and witty touch to the Irishman's Diary which transformed that column; Myles na Gopaleen, author of the famous Cruiskeen Lawn column, unique in

---

*At such times Smyllie occasionally recalled his early days in Sligo where his father had owned and edited a weekly newspaper. He and my wife's predecessors, journalistic colleagues, were friends of the family and relatives of the poet William Allingham, who lived at Ballyshannon — 'just up the road' as R. M. put it. Allingham, too, was a journalist — editor of Fraser's Magazine — and a friend of Dickens, Tennyson and other notables. Smyllie called him 'our most neglected poet'.

journalism; Alan Montgomery, regarded as the country's foremost Chief Reporter, son of the novelist Lynn Doyle and a later Editor; the author Brian Inglis, who began there as a junior reporter, the aforesaid 'Pussy' O'Mahony, general manager; assistant leader writers Jack White, Bruce Williamson and Lionel Fleming — and, of course, Alec Newman.

* *

"I would have been a film star but John Huston, the director, couldn't stand my Northern accent"
— Seamus Kelly (Quidnunc of the *Irish Times*) who had a bit part in Moby Dick.

* *

Patrick Campbell, a 6ft 5in eccentric and one of the best loved humorists, was derisively called 'The Hon' or 'The Hun' and later of course he became Lord Glenavy. It was amusing to listen to him with his slight stutter describing how once at a party he was introduced as 'the Venerable P-Patrick C-Campbell'. But it was in the Palace Bar that we heard him tell about his abdominal operation. "V-very embarrassing," he recalled. "Before the operation a f-fellow came along to my bed with a razor — a c-cut-throat type — the razor I mean. He pulled the bedclothes right down, undid my pyjamas, and brandished the razor. I had a terrible foreboding that he was about to perform some dr-dreadful rite. I was going to scream for help. Then he began to sh-shave me — you know, d-down there. Unbelievable. I didn't recognize myself afterwards — b-bare and innocent as a baby."

The Diary became a brilliant feature under Campbell's talents. He liked to relate tales of his off-duty alcoholic adventures with the Irish Naval Service. And of the day when in full uniform he called on R.M. at his office looking for a job. "The Editor gave me a d-dusty reception — told me he didn't require any lavatory attendants today, thank you."

Campbell won a much wider readership later with his *Sunday Times* column.

Chapter 7

THE GENIUS OF MYLES

The Brother's antics had them all 'in stitches'

In a corner of the Palace lounge one evening Smyllie was seen in deep conversation with a stranger — a middle-sized man whose old overcoat and battered soft hat gave him a nondescript appearance. Some fellow looking for a job perhaps? In fact it was the other way round — R.M. was trying to induce the stranger to work for him. Fortunately he succeeded. The man became celebrated and recognized as a great comic genius — Brian O'Nolan, whom the Editor persuaded to start the column which became so popular under the title Cruiskeen Lawn, and that was how Myles na Gopaleen — O'Nolan's pen-name — became for ever linked with the *Irish Times*.

O'Nolan, a civil servant in the Department of Local Government, had at the time just published an extraordinary novel *At Swim Two Birds* and Smyllie was struck by the man's outpouring of literary fireworks, comedy and invention. And his new column now was an astonishing mixture of satire, burlesque, fantasy and punning. Myles used words and phrases like a conjuror. Many of the garrulous characters whom he introduced, such as The Brother, Sir Myles (the Da) and the District Justice so seized people's imagination that they became almost real and they are still quoted today.

Three times a week for more than 25 years Myles — also known as Flann O'Brien — contributed the column which kept the whole country laughing. It was a nonsense column, yet it had everything — wide knowledge and originality mixed up with wit and ludicrous situations. The Brother, for example, is still an almost believable personality in Dublin talk: "The Brother had them all in stitches above in the digs the other night . . . The Brother got a Guard transferred — was lifting the little finger too much for The Brother's taste . . . " The Brother has in fact been turned into a one-man theatre show.

Imaginary adventures of the poets Keats and Chapman as portrayed by Myles were closely followed by readers — for example:

Chapman was much given to dreaming and often related to

Keats the strange things he saw when in bed asleep. On one occasion he dreamt that he had died and gone to heaven. He was surprised and rather disappointed at what he saw, for although the surroundings were most pleasant there seemed to be nobody about. The place seemed to be completely empty, and Chapman saw himself wandering disconsolately about looking for somebody to talk to. He suddenly woke up without solving this curious puzzle. "It was very strange," he told Keats. "I looked everywhere, but there wasn't a soul to be seen." Keats nodded understandingly. "There wasn't a sinner in the place," he said.

* *

"Hello, is that yourself? It's me. You're looking well. Don't hang up. I've got a great story for you . . . Hello . . . Hello . . ."
— A merry Myles na Gopaleen phoning editor
R.M. Smyllie from the Palace Bar.

* *

Myles — whose other aliases included George Knowall, Count O'Blather and Brother Barnabas — maintained constant war against clichés and 'gibberish' used in some official documents. A few examples from this Catechism of Cliché:

Take the word 'relegate'. To what must a person be relegated? *That obscurity from which he should never have been permitted to emerge.*

What may one do with a guess, provided one is permitted? *Hazard.*

And what is comment? *Superfluous.*

When was our friend born? *Not today or yesterday.*

What is he as good an Irishman? *As ever wore a hat.*

Where was our friend in 1916? *Under the bloody bed, like a lot more.*

But, like a lot more, Myles could become taciturn and moody. In the pub some people avoided getting into his company fearing he could be provoked into some quarrelsome scene.

In the office one evening Myles found himself in conversation with Seamus Laverty, a witty character and one of the paper's good sub-editors. Seamus, husband of Maura Laverty, the authoress of *Never No More* and other novels, was knowledgeable about economic affairs — or seemed to be. He could turn any conversation into a dispute about the country's finances. He had — or seemed to have — an astonishing memory for statistics and could recite Budget figures till the cows came home. At the same time something about his innocent gaze made one wonder. Then he announced 'a great idea' — he was writing a play that would cause a sensation — about economics. He smiled indulgently when we declared such a play would never succeed.

One evening he dropped a bulky manuscript in front of us and exclaimed, "There you are — my play. It's a send-up of all these economic clowns who are making such a balls-up of things. Read it — it's a knockout." We did read it — or anyway part of it. But it was heavy going — all talk by a series of characters, each attacking the others with figures and quotes from Budget speeches. Was Seamus serious one wondered, or was this all a leg-pull? There was no clue from that guileless expression.

Now unexpectedly he had Myles here in the office as his distinguished audience and after discoursing on his favourite topic he produced the manuscript. "There you are," he said. "It's all in there. Read my play on the subject. It makes it all clear as never before. Maybe you can influence your friends at the Abbey Theatre to put it on."

Seamus and Myles stood there looking each other straight in the eye. Neither man blinked! Well, hell's bells, I told myself. Greek meets Greek. It's all a gag — must be. Seamus is putting one over on the great man himself.

At last Myles lowered his gaze from this harmless-seeming colleague, took the manuscript, glanced at the first few pages, then said gravely, "Thank you. I will need some time, of course, to read it thoroughly. I will return it to you very soon."

To this day I'm still not sure whether the shameless Seamus had led us all up the garden.

Joseph and Margaret (née Beattie) Orr, parents of the author,
pictured on their wedding day.

Chapter 8

KIDNAPPED!

But Larry the missing man never said a word

One of the sub-editors on the *Irish Times* staff was an intriguing personality, Larry de Lacy. With strong Republican sympathies but not, of course, a member of the IRA he was not the sort of journalist then recruited to the paper but it was widely believed that Smyllie was behind his appointment. He never talked politics and he was a pleasant companion on our visits to the Palace or the Pearl bars. The IRA were active at the time and, after a widespread bombing campaign, many of their members had been rounded up and imprisoned. Inside the movement a relentless hunt for informers was going on.

One evening in the summer 1941 Milne said, "Have you seen Larry? He should have been in here an hour ago. He's never late." Larry didn't turn up that evening — or the next. There was no word of him at his residence or elsewhere. He had mysteriously vanished. His disappearance caused a sensation and rumours. Had he been abducted? Shot? Speculation swept the office and, indeed, the country for Larry, who had worked on papers in the south and west of Ireland, was well known.

It emerged eventually that he had been kidnapped, about the same time as Stephen Hayes, the then IRA chief of staff — who was Larry's brother-in-law. The kidnappings were part of an internal republican feud. Hayes was accused of being a traitor and was interrogated for several weeks about alleged contacts with members of the de Valera Government. Although still shackled with chains he managed one day to escape and gave himself up to police at Rathmines. He said that he had been tortured. Larry, who was held separately, was also interrogated but released. There were stories that he had been kept prisoner in hide-outs in the Dublin Mountains and other places.

Larry resumed work at the office as if nothing had happened. Not a word was said by anyone concerning this mystery which had kept everyone guessing for weeks. Larry said nothing. The Editor said nothing. Colleagues said nothing. Once when we were in the Palace he told me briefly about his former friendship with de Valera but soon changed the subject and did not refer to it again. He left the *Irish Times* a few years later and went to the *Drogheda Argus* as Editor.

It was said that after his kidnapping he always carried a revolver. There was continued speculation about him and the circumstances in which he joined the *Irish Times* staff. His background was recalled — he had been close to de Valera earlier, had accompanied him during an American fund-raising campaign reporting his speeches — some said helping in their compilation. He was talked of as perhaps a man who had been kidnapped in error.

Larry de Lacy, regarded as the 'mystery man' of the staff, died in 1973 at the age of 86.

*   *   *

The general public, of course, were unaware of the presence then in Ireland of German spy Dr Hermann Goertz, who had been parachuted from a Heinkel aircraft the previous year. Goertz had several meetings with Stephen Hayes with the aim of promoting sabotage and spying.

He and other spies were rounded up over a period and held in Athlone Prison. They included Ernst Weber-Drohl, Gunther Schuetz (also known as Hans Marschner), Werner Unland, Walter Simon (also known as Carl Andersen), Herbert Tributh, Willy Preetz (also known as Patrick Mitchell), Dieter Gartner, Jan Van Loon and Henry Obed.

Goertz, the most remarkable of the group, after being parachuted wandered about for four days, lost. He collapsed from hunger but eventually managed to reach Laragh, Co. Wicklow, and was given shelter by Mrs Iseult Stuart (daughter of the celebrated Maud Gonne MacBride) then the wife of the author Francis Stuart, who was in Germany at the time making broadcasts to Ireland.

The 'oddball' of the spies Ernst Weber-Drohl, lost his wireless set in the sea after a dinghy capsized when he was being landed from a U-boat. He turned out to be a former wrestler known as 'Atlas the Strong'. He was supposed to be conveying cash for the IRA. After his arrest he told a confused story about trying to contact his two children by a former Irish girl-friend. Most of these German agents were badly briefed and extraordinarily ignorant of Irish affairs. Goertz was the most intelligent of the lot — but even he didn't know that English currency was in use in Ireland. And when he was lost between Co. Meath and Co. Wicklow he actually called at a police station to ask for directions!

In the office there were stories of these spies and Smyllie, from his contacts, was aware of what was going on, but nothing could be published.

Chapter 9

'THE LADY ROSALEEN'

Midnight misadventure with The Senator

My 'digs' in Dublin were in Leeson Street, within walking distance of the office. The house was a large rambling place with a lot of stairs and a bewildering number of rooms. Breakfast was served in a large converted basement with a turf fire. Eight others were seated round a long table and I was asked to join them. Four were students, two were barmen, one worked in a store, and the other was a dealer of some kind. A lively lot — but the person who dominated the group was one of the students, nicknamed 'The Senator', a tall, well-dressed and confident figure, his thick reddish-brown hair splendidly groomed.

"Good-morning, you are most welcome," he said, rising majestically and he made the introductions with airy good humour. I learned that he had earned his nickname partly because of his seniority but mainly because of his knowledge of political affairs, his degree of authority and his ability to 'lay down the law'. He referred to Government ministers and members of the Dail by their first names and appeared to be acquainted with a great many of them. It emerged, too, that he had been a medical student for years and years and showed little sign of ever being anything else. Michael, one of the barmen, told me, "The Senator has bags of ready money and couldn't care less if he never qualifies. His people have a big farm in the Golden Vale, in County Tipperary. He's a bit of a boozer and always up to some lark or other — anything for a laugh with him."

Next morning there was a sample of this. As I was about to drink my cup of coffee I thought The Senator was observing me with a curious expression. I took just a sip of coffee. It had a bitter taste so the cup was left untouched. Just as well — I discovered later that he had tried one of his tricks — laced the newcomer's cuppa with Epsom salts.

Next day I went down early for breakfast and 'accidentally' dropped a spoonful of marmalade on his chair. But he spotted it and mopped the chair clean — with a page of the *Irish Times*. Cheeky beggar. He was a good fellow at heart though, and as a group we all got along well.

About 2.30 one morning on returning from the office I collided with two 'bodies' in the darkness of the hallway. There was an exclamation of alarm, a woman's frightened voice. A match was struck alight. It was The Senator with a red-haired girl. They had that been-on-the-town look.

"What the hell are you doing here at this time?" he demanded in an aggressive whisper as if I was an intruder.

I hissed back, "Daft question. I might ask you the same thing. However — good-night to you both."

The match burned out and The Senator said in another resounding whisper, "Ah, begob, what's the rush, come on up and we'll have a coupla jars, before you go on to bed" — and in the darkness Red Head started giggling.

Just then the lights were suddenly switched on and the landlady, in her dressing-gown, descended the stairs. She was carrying a poker.

"Jesus, Mary and Joseph — here comes Lady Macbeth," exclaimed The Senator. "Avaunt and quit my sight, let the earth hide thee" — and he struck an impressive, if a little unsteady, stage attitude.

But the landlady wasn't impressed. "What's going on here?" she demanded. "Who is this woman? How did she get in here?"

The Senator bowed low. "Allow me, ma'am, to present my fiancée, the Lady Rosaleen, who has come up from her family castle in the West to honour us all this day."

The landlady sniffed — "Family castle, Lady Rosaleen indeed. You mean some harpie you picked up in one of your low pubs down there in The Coombe. Get her out of my house this minute. And you yourself, sir, had better get out as well, and look smart about it."

The Senator began to bluster, but the landlady pushed them both to the door in determined fashion and banged it shut upon them with The Senator still protesting on the doorstep outside.

She turned back and for a moment I thought I was going to get an earful as well. But to my surprise she was half-smiling. "He's a great eejit that fellow," she said. "Too much money and no sense of responsibility. Everything's been too easy for that one — and I don't think much of his father either. He must be a fool as well."

After she had said good-night she turned back and added, "You needn't lose any sleep about The Senator. It's not the first time something like this has happened. He'll be back later on. You'll see."

She was right. He was — and as if nothing had ever happened. Quite a character The Senator. But he turned out to be a staunch friend.

Chapter 10

A COMMISSIONER!

"Damned embarrassing," said the Editor

It was difficult sometimes getting into the *Irish Times* office because of the masses of bicycles stacked in the front lobby. Petrol being scarce there were virtually no cars on the roads. Milne, the chief sub-editor, was devoted to his own constantly polished bike and aways carried it up to the subs' room and parked it where he could see it — near a small toilet, from which disturbing sounds occasionally emanated.

"Aye, it's a bonny hard job teaching auld dogs new tricks," said Milne one night. We were discussing the changes which we were trying to bring about in the handling of stories, lay-out of pages, and styles of headlines. He had been chief sub for many years and most of his staff — also 'old hands' — did not take kindly to any changes. Headlines were of the 'label' variety such as Sad Tragedy in City instead of Five Die in Car Crash, and so on. Stories often came up on proof twice the length stipulated. In the composing-room stories and headlines were desperately slow to materialize in type. Parts of stories went missing. So did captions for pictures. Making-up of pages was unbelievably slow and irksome. The foul-ups were aggravated by last-minute cuts in stories made by the censors.

One evening in the Pearl Bar Smyllie asked: "Well, how are things going?" It was the first time he had asked this and he possibly expected a bland non-committal answer. Instead he must have been taken aback to hear: "Things are not going well." He listened with seeming interest to a brief survey, asked a number of questions — and as a result of the chat and his promise to 'look into the situation' there seemed hope that something helpful might emerge. Perhaps he would now take a more active interest, assert his authority as Editor, transform the whole set-up. He could easily have done this and would have enjoyed it, too, in time. But no — instead he and the spokesman for the 'ginger' group had 'discussions' and one felt that in his easy-going style he had ducked out of a great opportunity to get involved and become the real boss. There would then be no need for a 'ginger' group.

A week or so later came the group's decision — one that astounded everybody, even Smyllie himself. An editorial 'Commissioner' was to be appointed.

A Commissioner! Such an appointment and such a title were unheard of in newspapers. Next day the name of the Commissioner was announced — Harold Brown, the sports editor. Another bombshell — the office and the city buzzed with the news. His brief was to 'move around and keep an eye on the working of every department in order to improve general efficiency.'

Harold himself admitted that he had been talked into taking the job. A cheerful and popular journalist he tried to make the best of things and even joked: "As Commissioner I think I should be given diplomatic status."

And Smyllie? The Editor was shaken — "Damned embarrassing," he growled. "It's making us a laughing stock in other offices."

Alec Newman's mildest words were, "Commissioner my arse — it sounds like a doorman. Will he wear a uniform?"

Milne the chief sub said, "Aye, wi' a title like that he'll have to wear the kilt."

Harold was given a specially-prepared office, and we 'drank' him into his new job one evening at the Pearl where Gus Weldon, the pub owner, and Edmund Honeyman,* then financial editor, gravely addressed him as, "Mr Commissioner, sir."

But in the office things went on just as before. And the situation was the subject of constant gossip at the Palace and the Pearl bars, and at the *Irish Times* Club — situated up several flights of stairs in Middle Abbey Street.

This club, which usually opened around midnight, was governed by a silent and unpredictable man who seemed to be for ever holding some secret fury just under control. He took orders sullenly and slammed down the glasses on the counter, glaring alarmingly. If something was said that annoyed him — even although he was not part of the conversation — he banged down the sliding shutter. Never mind if your drink was overturned — that was that — everybody out! Charming fellow.

Once on a night off I took The Senator along to the club. It was after midnight and Alec Newman, Harold Brown and others were already there. A dark-haired man whom I hadn't seen before was drinking at the end of the bar. To stir things up The Senator declared: "I hear Frank

---

* Edmund Honeyman, later a colleague on the *Daily Mail*, subsequently became a newspaper executive in Cape Town, South Africa.

Aiken is to tighten up the censorship." (Aiken at the time was Minister for Co-ordination of Defensive Measures and it was he who had set up the press censorship system, at Premier de Valera's instruction.)

* *

Fears of a German invasion led former Irish Premier de Valera to order the destruction of many 'foreign affairs' files in 1941.

* *

Aiken, The Senator went on, was doing a "great job". This remark was aimed at Newman and he gave me a nudge as he spoke.

"He certainly is not," objected Alec. "He's causing havoc in the office, and he's suppressing a lot of news which should be allowed into the paper. Is that not so, Mr Commissioner?"

Said Harold with some feeling: "The censors permit stories about the Russians massacring people in Poland, but we didn't see the same amount of space given to the massacring of Belfast people by the Germans, with almost a thousand people killed and whole rows of streets flattened in the air raids." (Harold was a Northerner).

At this stage The Senator began to make some reference to, "Cardinal MacRory, the Prods and the Jews" — but was never allowed to finish.

Suddenly the stranger at the end of the bar leapt off his stool and threw his pint glass at The Senator. In a moment the two were in a furious fight with fists and feet. As the rest of us tried to pull them apart the barman slammed down the shutter, flung open the door leading to the narrow flight of stairs, and roared: "Out, out, all of yez — out, or I'll call the Guards." And he somehow managed to shove the heaving mass through the door and down the stairs.

In the street the couple carried on with their fight, but as two cops approached the stranger hurried off quickly, calling out a final insult to The Senator. As we walked home Alec addressed Harold: "You're a bollocks. You should have arrested that man — you're the Commissioner."

Harold's regime as Commissioner never brought him satisfaction — nor did it do much good. He died tragically later. His body was found in his car, filled with exhaust fumes, in his garage after a function he had attended. It was believed that he had fallen asleep.

Chapter 11

'NED OF THE HILL'

Odd happenings on a quiet weekend

The Senator surprised me one day with an invitation to accompany him on a visit to his home the following weekend. "It's just down the line a bit," he said. By this he meant a journey by the Great Southern Railway to County Tipperary. As we left Broadstone, the then GSR terminus in Dublin, bound for Dundrum, The Senator explained: "It's a few miles beyond Thurles and before you come to Tipperary town."

Our steam train had been chugging along, at no great speed, for an hour and a half or so when suddenly it clanked to a standstill — in the middle of nowhere. Heads were poked out of carriage windows and then somebody shouted: "They're cleaning out the engine." Because of the 'Emergency' there was little coal for the railways, so substitutes had to be used. These choked up the locomotives' fire-boxes. Drivers and their mates had to stop and 'clean out'.

"We may have a few delays like this," grinned The Senator.

"What substitutes are being used?" I asked.

"Turf and wood — and a new kind of fuel they've discovered — a mixture of tar and some other stuff. It's supposed to a big secret." At that time 'mountains' of turf were stacked in Phoenix Park, coal being in short supply.

It was almost an hour before we started off again. More slowly than before. We stopped again — three times. The locomotive crew climbed down and went foraging for wood. Some of the passengers, ourselves included, got out of the carriages to help. "This is the easy part," said the loco men. "The worst job is cleaning out the fire-box."

We arrived at our destination four hours late and were met at the station by a man with a pony and trap.

"Hello, Tom. Been waiting long?" said The Senator.

"No, sir," the man smiled an obvious white lie. "I hope the journey from Dublin wasn't too unpleasant."

For half an hour or so we were trotted through wooded countryside surrounded by hills. Tom entertained us with a story about a train which had recently been reported 'lost' on the GSR line because of the

48

fuel difficulties. Another train had taken 14 hours on a 50-mile journey. Eventually we entered a narrow drive and then our trap pulled up outside a large Georgian house. The Senator was home — but he looked nervous. As Tom took our belongings the front door opened and two elderly look-alike ladies came to the top of the steps to greet us.

"Meet my mother and Aunt Juliet," said The Senator. Shaking hands with me the mother said, "Ah, so you managed to get here, after all. You're very welcome. Travelling is such an awful problem now." Aunt Juliet chimed in with: "Do come in and have a sundowner, and the house-boys will look after your kit."

Sundowners, house-boys, kit — what did she mean? It was a shabby old house with an air of neglect about the big hall and rooms.

"Where's the boss? Aloft in the look-out, I suppose," said The Senator addressing his mother.

"Yes, he'll be down for a whiskey* and sparkler with us, and then we'll have dinner. You must be exhausted after such a tedious journey."

Said Aunt Juliet: "You must travel by prahu next time — much faster." The Senator winked, enjoying my bewilderment.

Over drinks and later at dinner things became a little clearer. The look-out was an observatory which the father had rigged up in an attic. He had knocked a hole in the roof to accommodate a large telescope of his own construction and he spent half his nights surveying the stars and making notes.

We went up to the look-out with him that night. As he pointed out some of the great constellations he said dramatically: "Behold the envoys of the beauty of the universe. But the stars are hostile tonight. Ned must be cross with us. I feel it. We'll have to get him a drink." He produced a bottle of whiskey and four glasses — one of which he put to the side — "for Ned."

"Who the hell is Ned?" I whispered to The Senator.

"Tell you later," he said.

Then the old man began singing, "Eamonn a' Chnuic." I recognized the tune but not the words. Each time he refilled our glasses he said, "Good luck, Ned." Sometimes he said, "There's always a place for you here if you ever need it."

And so to bed happy — but puzzled. Next morning The Senator explained. "The boss thinks Ned of the Hill is the cause of all our problems."

Whiskey is the Irish and US spelling. *Whisky* is the Scottish spelling.

"For heaven's sake — who is Ned of the Hill?"

"Ever heard of a rapparee?" grinned The Senator. "Ned was Eamonn O Riain an officer of the Jacobite army. After their defeat and the siege of Limerick in 1691 he took to the hills and lived in a mountain cave near here. He made raids on the English planters in these parts. He was later betrayed and murdered. The boss thinks Ned is still plundering this district. He thinks Ned needs to be placated now and again."

At first I thought The Senator was spinning one of his tall stories. But that afternoon we went riding and found a cave in the hills near Cappagh White which Ned was believed to use as his hiding place.

The Senator explained that his father had been a planter in Malaysia. "I was born out there," he said. "Mother and Aunt Juliet are twins and have always been inseparable. Aunt Juliet lived with Mum and the boss. Juliet had a love affair out there with a chap she met in Singapore. They had planned to marry but Juliet had a breakdown — she couldn't bear to think of being parted from Mum. After that she became a bit funny. Now she imagines they're still living out East, talks about sundowners and prahus and so forth. Prahus are boats. She thinks people here should be using them."

It was late when we got back to the old house. The mother said, a little sadly: "Pity you didn't get back earlier. Rosemary came over and was here for tea." Said The Senator: "Very sorry to have missed her" — but the glance he gave made me wonder.

As we sat in the train next day on our way back to Dublin the weekend visit began to seem to me like a dream. The lonely old house with its strange characters. The father with his midnight boozing in the attic, star-gazing and raving about a bygone bandit. The eccentric Aunt Juliet living in her private world of the past. The mother, presenting a brave front in a crazy situation. And, to cap it all, the train journey, where one got out and looked for wood to get the engine running. What a performance!

The Senator interrupted my thoughts — "I think they would like me and Rosemary to get hitched. She lives near our place. Mum's very fond of her. She's a smashing girl all right — but I've no intention of getting married."

He gazed out of the window for a minute, then went on: "I like women, you bet, in the plural. Love them and leave them is my motto. Gather ye rosebuds while ye may — and all that stuff. Marriage is too high a price to pay for the pleasure I seek."

He laughed and continued: "It's all a con — a trap. Sex and marriage are merely Nature's device to get two people together to perpetuate the species. The love angle is a confidence trick. The trouble with women is they take you over and smother you. They use their wiles to make you conform to their ways. Before you know it you've become just like a piece of furniture around the house. I want to remain a free man."

That night back in Dublin we went out for a few pints. "Great to be back — good luck," said The Senator raising his glass — "and thanks for going down there with me."

Despite his devil-may-care veneer it was clear he shrank from facing his occasional visits home. Now, back in Dublin, he had recovered his good spirits.

Chapter 12

ECONOMIC PLAN!

'Everybody must go to bed for a week'

"Well, here's one thing that the censor canny kill," said Milne one evening when some copy arrived on his desk. It was an official hand-out for publication next day. At a time when tea and sugar were rationed — £1 per pound for tea on the black market — and when bread was scarce, this official statement urged housewives: 'Go easy on bread. Cut down on waste. Make full use of crusts, cold potatoes and left-over porridge.'

Declared Milne: "My wife will no be pleased wi' that advice. There's nae waste in our house, and never any stirabout left over."

The oldest sub-editor on the staff John Bunyan, who remembered all about the First World War, exclaimed: "You can't get cocoa or oranges or butter. Everything is too dear. The Brits are starving us out because we won't let them use our ports."

"Nonsense," said Seamus Laverty, "it's a problem of economics and necessity. There are now nearly 70,000 people unemployed in the Republic. Another 130,000 have gone to England to work in munitions and other jobs. Anyway, you can always eat pigeon pie."

Seamus was referring to another story which the censor had just okayed. It said that a big 'traffic in pigeons' was going on. The birds were being bought by Dublin housewives for three shillings each. In addition, loads of 3,000 at a time were being sent to Britain every day.

Bunyan retorted: "I'd rather starve than eat filthy rotten pigeons. Sure they'd poison you. They live on all sorts of rubbish."

But Seamus was off again on the social and economics trail — "The cost of living is today twice as much as it is in England, although England is at war and we're neutral. More than 70,000 Dublin people, including many large families, are living in one-room dwellings in rotten tenement buildings. The government should give decent family allowances for these people."

"No, no, no," declared Milne. "They'd only fritter away the money on drink."

"Splendid," cried Alec Newman who had just entered the room. "I feel like having a couple of jars — who's coming across to the Pearl?"

By coincidence that night Myles na Gopaleen in his column suggested a solution for the Republic's wartime problems. Needless to say, 'The Brother' had come up with another ingenious idea:-

'We all go to bed for a week every month. Every single man, woman and child in the country. Cripples, drunks, policemen, watchmen — everybody. Nobody is allowed to be up. No newspapers, buses, pictures or any other class of amusement allowed at all. No matter who you are you must go to bed for a week.

'You see, when nobody is up you save clothes, shoes, rubber, petrol, coal, turf, timber and everything we're short of. And food, too, remember. What makes you hungry? It's work that makes you hungry. If nobody's up there's no need for anybody to do any work. In a year you'd save a quarter of everything, and that would be enough to see us right.'

The 'Plain People of Ireland' — as Myles called them — were indeed tussling with the harsh effects of rationing in that year 1941 and defence forces were being mobilized to repel an attack — from whatever source. "Who are we neutral against?" was the cynical question often asked then.

In this dangerous situation men of the Republic's small, unprepared regular army looked sinister in their German-style steel helmets. The choice of these helmets had been made in peacetime. They were scrapped later and substituted by the more familiar 'tin hats'.

Smyllie's friends at the time included some remarkable characters. One of these was David Lubbock Robinson to whom he introduced me one day. Robinson, who had a patch over one eye, greeted R.M. jovially with: "Ah, Bertie, what big scoop are you chasing today? What waste-paper baskets have you been rummaging through this time?"

Robinson, an elderly, dapper type, seemed to know everyone of importance and after he had left I was curious to learn more about him.

Said Smyllie: "You'd never believe that chap once served in the British Army, won the DSO for gallantry — and then joined the IRA! It was an enormous sensation at the time. Robinson was later interned, but years afterwards was nominated as a Senator. Some of his friends regarded him as a renegade. But he could be described as an idealist — certainly a gentleman."

Robinson, the British Army hero turned Sinn Feiner, died in 1943.

Why had Senator Robinson referred to scoops and "rummaging through waste-paper baskets?" Smyllie then told of an ingenious bit of detective work and, as a change from the ordinary, one suddenly saw him in the role of Sherlock Holmes.

"The Senator," he said, "was referring to a scoop we had in the *Irish Times* during a big row that occurred in the Fianna Fail party over taking the Oath of Allegiance in the Dail. I had been visiting friends at Enniskerry. Afterwards when I arrived at the Powerscourt Arms Hotel to catch the late bus to Dublin three prominent Dail deputies were at the bus stop. We exchanged greetings but the three seemed reticent and ill at ease. When the bus came along they hastily said goodbye and jumped on board.

"Instead of getting on the bus I went into the hotel, had a brandy, and asked the proprietor, whom I knew, if the three politicians had been there that day. Yes, he said, they had been conferring for over three hours — in a summer-house in the garden. We went out to the summer-house, and there in a waste-paper basket were piles of torn-up notepaper. I asked the hotel owner to bring out a bottle of brandy, a pot of paste, and a few large sheets of paper.

"It was a long job, but we had the bottle, and when the jigsaw of notes was put together there were the names of a proposed new government. It caused a sensation when we published the list and the story of the conspiracy. It threw all parties into a turmoil. They were at each other's throats."

Smyllie would never have told such a story concerning himself if, say, sitting in the midst of a crowd in the Palace or the Pearl. There, as always, he sat drinking, smoking, listening and observing, his eyes shrewd behind his horn-rimmed glasses. Occasionally he would throw in a good-humoured comment or joke.

But if riled he could at times be unpleasant, even unfair. That side of his make-up was shown once about the middle of the war after he had acquired a weekend cottage to relax near the golf course he loved at Delgany in Co. Wicklow. At that time some branch offices had been closed as an economy measure.

One correspondent was transferred to Dublin and given a staff job. After a few weeks this man bought a large house along with some land, livestock and a swimming pool near the picturesque Glen o' the Downs. He and his family settled there and he travelled to and from the office each day. It seemed idyllic.

But one weekend Smyllie was cycling back from the golf club when he encountered on the country road his staff man — on horseback! It would be difficult to say which man was the more taken aback.

"In the name of God, man, what are you doing on a bloody horse?" R.M. demanded. He wasn't in a good mood. The unfortunate staffer, who had no idea this was Smyllie territory, explained about buying the house.

"You mean that big place up above the Glen?" asked R.M.

Sitting on his horse the staffer gazed down at his Editor and the old bike. An embarrassing situation and he managed: "Do you live near here, then, Bertie?"

R.M. growled: "Yes, in that old cottage over there. Well, see you Monday, I suppose." And he got on his bike.

Shortly afterwards, as part of another economy drive, the staffer found himself out of a job. He got temporary work on another paper the *Evening Mail*, but soon afterwards, with loan repayment problems, he had to sell his property at a big loss and leave Dublin.

* *

"I tell you a secret — I know the exact location (pointing to a wall-map) in the USSR where there is much gold. You and I are now the only two people who know!"

— Russian Ambassador Anatoli Kaplin
during an interview.

* *

One day I had a visit from my old pal George — "Thought I'd come down from Belfast and let you buy me a juicy Dublin steak," he grinned. That evening at the Dolphin he said, "I had to see the bright lights again after the black-outs." He hadn't changed and was soon telling me about a girl with whom he had spent some time in Londonderry.

"I promised to look her up," he said and he produced a page of a newspaper. The girl's name and address, written in bright red lipstick, covered the entire page. "She's got a fine pair of fetlocks."

It was a Dublin address. "So that's why you're here, you old devil," I accused him. "She must have made a big impression."

"Where is this place?" said George indicating the lipstick.

"I'll show you after we've had a few pints and a meal. Better build yourself up — you may need it in that area."

Later I escorted him to the district — Summerhill. Not the most salubrious part of the city — and the address he sought turned out to be a run-down tenement, the hallway in darkness. As with all the neighbouring tenement houses the front door lay wide open. We stepped inside and as I lit a match a couple of figures lying under a stairway half-rose in sudden alarm. We ascended the stairs and George knocked at a door on the first floor landing.

"Next floor up," an old woman wheezed in response to his inquiry. We stumbled on our way.

"Wonder if this is wise — let's have another drink," I suggested, "and we'll come back tomorrow."

Too late — George had already knocked at a door. There was a roar from inside, the door was flung open and a tough looking fellow in shirt sleeves, bottle in hand, stood swaying in candle-light. "What do you bastards want here?" he shouted.

"Sorry, sir. Think we have the wrong address," said George, backing away as we saw an agitated female figure in the background. A yell of, "I know why you're here," was followed by a stream of abuse and a bottle smashed against the wall as we made our way down the dark stairs.

"Messy situation that," said George as we walked towards the club. "She was a very attractive, well-spoken girl and gave me to understand that she had her own flat. Never thought things would turn out like that. Must be more careful in future."

He obviously took his own advice because a few years later I had a letter from Perth — he had met an Australian girl, a wealthy heiress, and they had just got married Down Under where her family had large properties. He was to help in their management. Good old George — all's well that ends well.

Chapter 13

EDITOR'S BATTLE

Paragraph 'cut' that caused fury

The most memorable period of Smyllie's editorship was his long and unrelenting battle with the Irish censorship which at one stage, he visualized, looked like landing him in prison.

R.M. accepted, as he had to, the fact of neutrality, but never once relaxed his efforts to get as much news as possible past the censors. He saw that as his prime duty. "People who buy the paper are entitled to get the news," he said. "Any official can strike out news. Our job is to get it into the paper and we can best do that by presenting stories fairly and straightforwardly."

He had frequent conflicts with the censorship. Some of these occurred over reports which in themselves seemed trivial at the time. One item of only twelve lines with a small headline 'Bruce Hobbs Gets the MC' was found to have been completely deleted when the proof came back from censorship. But the 'killing' of this one-paragraph story caused anger throughout the office.

The story seemed harmless enough. It read: 'Acting Capt. Bruce Hobbs, the steeplechase rider, who won the Grand National on Battleship, has been awarded the MC. Bruce was only 17 when he won the National. The same year his back was broken in a fall at Cheltenham and it was thought he would never ride again but he made a remarkable recovery. He has been on service more than three years in the Middle East where he has twice been wounded.'

Staffmen denounced the anonymous official at the Castle who had blue-pencilled such a news item. Many of them recalled backing Battleship in the National. "How can Battleship's jockey receiving an award affect the country's neutrality?" they demanded.

The young Bruce Hobbs and his gallant little horse had especially gained everyone's admiration. The 11-year-old Battleship stood just over 15 hands high and weighed under 1,000 lbs. Despite his slight physique he carried 11st 6lbs in that race at Aintree, yet beat a field of 35 — which included horses of much greater size and, it was thought, stamina. A son of Man of War he was the only horse to win the 'double'

— both the American Grand National and the Aintree National. He had many Irish backers and young Hobbs won great acclaim for his bravery and determined riding after the fall at Cheltenham which threatened his career.

Smyllie brandished the proof showing the deleted story — there were eight heavy blue-pencilled lines through the brief paragraph. "It hasn't just been cut," he raged, "it's been massacred. The individual who did that should be ashamed."

There was a row, too, over a Dail speech by Mr Oliver Flanagan, who declared that many members of the Republic's forces were 'deserting' and joining the Royal Air Force. He asked: "How can we keep an army here if the British Air Force is issuing members of the Irish Army with travel permits?"

He also claimed that 'high officers of the Irish Army' had sons serving in the British armed forces, and he asked: "How can we expect good service from such officers?" These statements were suppressed. Other items deleted referred to Irish soldiers returning on leave from Britain wearing 'civvies' provided for them at British ports of departure.

The censors killed any references to IRA internees. At one stage 390 IRA men were interned, but de Valera refused to yield to hunger strike action and two men, Jack McNeela and Tony Darcy died in the early period of the war. Earlier de Valera had said on radio, "If we released them we would fail as a government . . . if they do not come off the hunger strike they will die." The hunger strike as a weapon withered after that.

In this hush-hush atmosphere the Republic was repeatedly swept by rumours — parachute 'landings', submarines being refuelled at Western rendezvous, even invasion attempts. Some of these stories originated among the people of assorted nationalities thronging the Shelbourne, the Hibernian and other Dublin hotels.

One day as The Senator and I headed towards the Shelbourne for a drink he suddenly stopped, contorted his features in fiendish style and exclaimed, "Ach, ve are two German spies, hein? Ven at ze Shelbourne ve arrife ve take ze pizz out of ze odder guests — zut!"

"OK, meinherr."

The Senator produced a couple of cheroots, we lit up, went inside and he demanded, "ze best Rhenish wine."

"Just one snag about this spy lark," I muttered to him, "I really want a pint of you know what."

The Senator, who had now adorned himself with a monocle —

really a large key-ring — retorted, "Silence, swine, ve must not of ourselves be always thinking. Our glorious duty now is uber alles de vaterland," — he jumped to attention and clicked his heels loudly so that people turned and stared.

"Watch it," I warned. "You'll bust our cover or — worse still — maybe do yourself an injury."

A few fellows we knew entered the bar and, at once twigging the situation, joined happily in the act. And as others arrived our area was soon in a jabbering, arm-waving uproar with waiters looking anxious and some of the real foreigners in the place casting angry glances and exchanging looks of disgust.

Among the English 'refugees' there at the time were some who, it was known, openly supported the Union of Fascists whose leader Sir Oswald Mosley had been arrested in Britain under Section 18 B of the Emergency Powers regulations and interned. We met a few of them on this occasion. One — Sylvia, a novelist and a supporter of Hitler — told me that she had had to leave her flat in London because, she said, she was 'being watched'.

She began relating a story about her 'clandestine activities' on the Continent — how she and some of her friends had been working against the 'corruptive regime' of King Carol of Rumania. "We forced him to abdicate and now Rumania has joined the Axis," she boasted.

She was one of those 'aggressive' talkers and I found myself forced into a slow retreat as she kept moving loquaciously forward. We had traversed in this way half the width of the room when, having backed into a side table, I was forced to stop and she unintentionally trod on me.

"Ah, I am standing on your foot," she exclaimed cheerfully.

"Oh, no, not at all — my fault entirely. But you must excuse me. I have to telephone my office."

Actually I wanted to rejoin The Senator, who had now removed his 'monocle' and appeared to be undergoing admonition from a management official. But then they were shaking hands and he greeted me with a grin and, "All quiet now on the Western front. The spies have run for cover."

That was a light interlude during a critical period. The British, American, German, Italian and Japanese diplomatic missions in Dublin were very active then concerning supplies, alleged breaches of neutrality, US demands for the use of Irish ports, and many other subjects, including radio transmissions from the German Embassy. In consequence there were frequent meetings between Prime Minister de

Valera and Joseph Walshe, Secretary of the Department of External Affairs, on the Irish side, and the three main diplomats Sir John Maffey (Britain), Mr David Gray (United States) and Herr Edouard Hempel (Germany).

But, unsuspected at the time by the outside world and indeed by people in the Republic, there were secret contacts and 'arrangements' with Britain and the United States on some aspects of defence.

For example, supplies of certain classes of arms were being received from the United Kingdom. On the other hand, a number of RAF pilots and air crews who had been interned at the Curragh military camp were, after a time, driven across the Border into Northern Ireland and quietly restored to the British.

Chief of Military Intelligence — then known as G2 — was a remarkable personality Colonel Dan Bryan, a gifted officer esteemed by his British and American counterparts and consulted on occasion by Premier de Valera. A 'man of secrets' he carried a burden of responsibility then concerning the country's neutrality as well as its defences. But, no seeker after publicity later, his secrets died along with him.

"Dan Bryan was a figure to put into the shade even the more elaborate fantasy figures of such novelists as John Le Carre," commented a well-known former officer in the Irish Army who served under him during the 'Emergency' years. "He and his staff were on top of their job at that dangerous time — the highlight of his military career — when many of the secret burdens of neutrality rested on his shoulders and on those of Joseph Walshe and Fred Boland, of the Department of External Affairs. He was an original — unforgettable."

*   *   *

As a little light relief from office work Noel Fee and I decided one day: What a good idea it would be to take over a weekly newspaper. This occurred while we were reducing the stocks of Guinness at the Pearl.

Noel, a sub-editor on the *Irish Times* and a very droll character indeed, suddenly observed: "I hear that the *Drogheda Argus* is up for sale." He gazed over his glass — "Somebody could make a bloody good thing outa the *Drogheda Argus*."

"You mean you could?"

"No, I mean we could."

This was interesting — Noel must be rolling in it, I thought, when he talks so coolly about buying — buying — a newspaper.

"I began on a weekly paper," I said helpfully.

"So did I — in Longford," said Noel. "We both know the drill. What about it? With your money and my undoubted genius we couldn't go wrong."

"You've got it the wrong way round — have you got a copy of the *Argus*, by the way?"

"No," said Noel. "There isn't any *Argus* at the moment."

"How can we buy a newspaper that doesn't exist?"

Noel explained that publication of the paper had been suspended for some years because of strong competition from the other local paper. "Let's go up there and scout around and maybe we'll buy it," he said. "It should be going cheap. We will become the Rothermeres of Ireland."

"Right," I said. "But first I want to have a bash at that story up in County Monaghan — the cinema that won't allow any kissing or cuddling by courting couples."

"That's alliteration," said Noel.

"They don't allow that either."

It turned out to be an amusing story. A fellow taking his girl to this cinema was not allowed to sit with her. He had to sit with other men on one side of the hall. The girl had to sit with other females on the opposite side. But married couples were allowed to sit together. Big deal.

"They must be a funny lot up there," grinned Noel. "They were never as careful as that in Longford."

The story, helped with comments from local picture-goers, went down well with the Sunday papers. But the *Irish Times* gave it only ten lines with a tiny headline.

And so to Drogheda — first to a solicitor's office. "Where are you from?" asked a senior partner who, we had been told, acted for the owner of the *Argus*.

But the solicitor seemed more anxious to find out all about us than to volunteer any information himself. Our next contacts were of little help but one did mention a man said to have 'business associations with the owner'.

We found this man living alone in a cottage. I thought he looked a bit strange — and in fact we were in for a shock. As we were explaining our business he beckoned us inside. In the hall he turned upon us suddenly and demanded: "Have you made your peace — have you been saved?"

Noel said: "Come on now, have a bit of sense, for heaven's sake."

But the man glared at us and shouted: "For heaven's sake — you are sinners both of you. Down on your knees while I pray for your immortal souls." And he flopped down in the hall, his hands clasped.

Noel and I stared in alarm as he launched into an incoherent series of instructions to the Almighty. "Exit pronto," I muttered to Noel and we edged towards the door and got outside.

Said Noel: "I think we need a drink. Whoever told us of that chap was having us on."

In the nearby pub the owner shook his head as we mentioned having called at the cottage. "Poor fellow's suffering from schizophrenia," he said. "There's a lot of it about." The pub owner turned out to be a mine of information — the paper we had come to buy, he said, had already been sold! He was right and — another shock — it's first editor was to be none other than our former colleague of the *Irish Times*, Larry de Lacy.

"Well I'll be damned," said Noel. "Larry kept very quiet, didn't he? He must have known about our trip to Drogheda all the time. He's been laughing up his sleeve at us two eejits wandering round the town trying to buy a newspaper that had been sold already. Never mind — good luck to old Larry. He'll need it with newsprint now so scarce."

In fact the *Argus* changed hands a few times during later years. And in those years some well-known personalities served on its staff. They included Ted Nealon, from Sligo, who later became a government minister, and at least three reporters who became editors of national newspapers — Joe Kennedy, Michael Hand and Kevin Marron. Patsy McArdle, one of the country's best known press correspondents, worked there for a time.

But perhaps the best known character to have been on the *Argus* in de Lacy's time was a youngster named O'Mahony. From being jack of all trades on the paper he eventually blossomed into the famous comedian Dave Allen. Son of the celebrated 'Pussy' O'Mahony, former general manager of the *Irish Times*, it's no wonder, some people say, that Dave became such a favourite on TV and stage. 'Pussy's' eccentricities were the amused talk of Dublin newspaper offices, and Dave is said to have based some of his funniest stories on his dad's legendary adventures.

One of these stories — legendary or not — concerned 'Pussy's' wooden leg. His foot got caught in a lift and, it was said, he amputated it with a penknife. He got his nickname because one night when drunk he took the saucer of milk which had been left for the office cat.

Chapter 14

PADDY AND PETER

Eccentric poet and crafty matchmaker

Only a few weeks after our effort to become newspaper proprietors there was another barmy adventure — this time with the poet and novelist Paddy Kavanagh. He had demanded in his gruff style: "Why didn't you tell me you were going up there? You know damn well that I come from that area and could have helped you. Let's have a drink."

In the pub he surprised me by saying that he still owned a farm in Co. Monaghan. He had lived there with his brother until a few years previously, he said, then decided to move to Dublin 'to follow a literary career.' He said he had walked the 50 miles or so to Dublin. But he was not having much success in his efforts to make money and get himself known by selling articles and short stories to Dublin editors.

He fiercely criticized the 'illiterate' standards of Dublin journalists in general — and the 'hostility' of Smyllie and 'dreariness' of the *Irish Times* in particular. He grew irritated when I suggested that the *Irish Times* could scarcely be regarded as dreary with such writers as Patrick Campbell, Myles, Jack White, Tony Gray and Tony Olden.

"If you were in my shoes you would see things differently," he said bitterly. "Dublin's a malignant town. Sean O'Casey was right about its taunts and slights and slanders. It would turn a decent man into a charlatan."

Kavanagh went on: "The decentest man I've met here in Dublin isn't an Irishman at all — he's an Englishman, Sean Betjeman. We're great friends."

In fact he was referring to John Betjeman, who was then a press attaché at the British Embassy in Dublin but who, years later became Poet Laureate. Betjeman developed a liking for the outspoken Paddy and even recruited him into playing cricket for an Embassy XI one day. He was one of the first to appreciate Paddy's poetic gifts, and Paddy composed a poem in honour of the Betjemans' daughter Candida on her first birthday.

In the pub we were joined by Tony Olden, an *Irish Times* sub — a gifted chap who, tragically, died at an early age. Kavanagh talked so eloquently about Co. Monaghan and its characters that in an 'inspired' moment Tony and I agreed to take 'a run up there just for the gas' and to visit his farm.

Paddy took us first to a pub — which was also a funeral undertakers. Then he insisted we cycle to Carrickmacross where we got involved with successive groups of 'cattle men' and 'pig men'. They all seemed to be called McMahon — "Oh, this is great McMahon country," explained Paddy. Most illuminating.

"Everybody in these parts is a dealer, and those not dealers are smugglers," he said. "You can get anything around here — anything. Sometimes I'm sorry I ever moved to Dublin — but I had to — I'm a poet, and they don't think much of bloody poets up here."

We finished up in Dundalk — a succession of taverns — Paddy growing ever taller, wider and louder — meeting more and more 'pig men' and 'cattle men' all called McMahon. Well after midnight a figure was observed climbing the steps of a big hotel and banging on the heavy door.

No response from inside, and as the knocking continued a garda on night duty approached. "Now, sir, what's all this row? Why are you hammering away at that door at this time of the morning?"

"Want to get into the hotel. Want to spend the night here."

"Well, sir, you won't spend the night in there — that's the Bank of Ireland you're trying to get into. The hotel's further along the street — come along with me."

We never visited Paddy's farm — the object of the pilgrimage.

Kavanagh — like some others who were not all that popular or highly regarded during their lifetime — has grown hugely and deservedly in reputation, stature and appreciation since his death. Many now consider him the finest poet since W.B. Yeats. Just one verse from his salute *Candida* — for John Betjeman's daughter:

Candida is one today — What is there that one can say?
One is where the race begins, or the sum that counts our sins;
But the mark time makes tomorrow shapes the cross of joy or
                                                            sorrow.

And a verse from his poem *If Ever You Go to Dublin Town* — which shows that at times he could be his own severest critic:

Go into a pub and listen well if my voice still echoes there.
Ask the men what their grandsires thought, and tell them to
                                                    answer fair.
Oh — he was eccentric. Fol dol the di do,
He was eccentric I tell you!

*   *   *

And then there was an encounter with a marriage match-maker . . . In the forecourt of a hotel I saw guests fastening a placard on the back of bridal car: 'Thank you — Peter Cupid'.

Peter Cupid? What did it mean?

"He's the fellow who matched them up," they cried. "Peter the match-maker. Ah, sure Peter's a great man for the job."

A few days later I found 'Mr Cupid' in County Monaghan — Peter McKenna, a dealer by trade who did match-making 'for the fun of it and for the merry-making'. He had hitched up many couples in his career.

* *

"I can't really support her if we marry — but I can get her a better-paid job"
— Young farmer during negotiations with a match-maker.

* *

And now he was at a critical point in his latest 'job'. Some weeks previously he had been approached by a farmer's daughter who wanted to go to a dance but had no partner at the time. Peter engineered an introduction between the girl and a young farmer. The two enjoyed the evening together at the dance and then started 'going steady'.

The big night when the 'match' was to be arranged was now imminent and Peter allowed me to go along as silent observer in the background. The meeting took place in the private sitting-room of a hotel. The young man, accompanied by his parents and the girl, with her parents, all attended. Peter took charge of the proceedings, keeping up a flow of conversation.

The man and his parents sat at one side of a table, the girl with hers at the other. Peter, seated at the end, reviewed how the couple's friendship had blossomed so that now they wished to marry. "They believe," he said, "and I believe so, too, that they can be very happy together." Then, very seriously, he went on: "But marriage, as we know, has a practical aspect as well as a romantic side. If these two young people can start out on a solid basis prospects for their future life together will be even brighter."

Looking at the parents in turn he said: "I feel sure you will agree with that." They all murmured approval. Sitting in the background I thought Peter was doing a good job.

The young farmer's parents without embarrassment then asked questions about the girl's 'fortune' — the kind of dowry by way of money or property she might bring to her husband. In their turn the girl's people inquired about the value of the other party's farm, the amounts and variety of livestock. For more than an hour the talks went on. There were repeated references to large sums — many thousands of pounds in terms of property, livestock and bank balances. At first sight these parties did not strike one as being so wealthy, and the matter-of-fact way in which they referred to such amounts of money and possessions was an eye-opener.

Under Peter's guidance the discussions went cordially, the 'match' was made, the wedding date was fixed, there were handshakes all round. Then drinks were produced by Peter and the young couple, now hand in hand, were toasted by all in turn.

Later when I commented to Peter on the apparent ease with which the 'match' had been arranged he smiled knowingly: "Each party had a good idea well beforehand of the other's standing. Things went easily because the discussions merely confirmed what they already believed. Country folk are pretty shrewd."

But not all Peter's match-making efforts were so successful. One ended very abruptly. He explained: "That match was for a man of almost 60 with £30,000 in the bank and 40 acres of land. I told him I knew someone who I believed would be just the one for him. I said I would arrange a meeting. 'What about the matter of her dowry?' I then asked him. He replied: 'Ah, sure she needn't worry about that if I think she's the right girl.'

"When we all met the couple were nervous and tongue-tied. I took them into the lounge of an hotel. They thawed out and began chatting freely. The rich suitor grinned at me and seemed delighted with my choice.

"I felt relieved. All appeared to be going well. I invited them to have a drink. The girl asked for a gin and lime. That's when everything went down the drain. The man's face suddenly lost its affable look. He looked at his watch, jumped to his feet, said he had to go, and would see me later. Then he strode out of the hotel. It transpired that he strongly disapproved of women drinking alcohol. The girl was a bit shaken at first but later laughed about the incident."

Peter told me of a young farmer who contemplated marrying the daughter of a neighbouring farmer. Then he found out that the girl was pregnant by someone else. Furious, he went to her father. "The match is off," he stormed. "I've been deceived. Your daughter's in the family way."

Replied the father soothingly: "Ah, sure, don't worry. Only a little bit."

Chapter 15

EDITOR v. CENSORS

'All right — let them send me to prison'

Back in the *Irish Times* office the 'battle' was still going on. I still have in my possession a mass of proofs showing the 'treatment' that stories received at the hands of the censors. When finished with, the proofs were thrown into a big waste-paper basket — there were so many of them. More than once Alec Newman told me he thought it was a pity that they should be dumped like that as it was the first time such a thing had happened in the office. "Take them away," he said. "They are evidence of how news is dealt with at times like this — write about them later."

Well, here they are — some of them — in the pages that follow! Details and photographs of 'cuts' and alterations made by the wartime censors are clearly shown. They are in their way historic, as evidence of what can happen to news reports in wartime even in neutral countries. But they represent only a fraction of what actually occurred. Early in the war Frank Aiken, the Minister for Co-ordination of National Defence, served the newspapers with a list of directives. Editors were forbidden to leave blank spaces in a page. So Smyllie had a picture of the Statue of Liberty prepared, ready to publish in place of a severely cut editorial if things went too far.

R.M. made little attempt to conceal his efforts to beat the censors at every stage. He took the view at the time that under Aiken the officials in their 'over-anxiety to be neutral' were inadvertently leaning towards Germany and her Axis partners. It angered him, for example, that in an obituary of Judge John McGonigal the censors deleted the fact that his youngest son Eoin was a lieutenant and was killed in Libya — at a time when many hundreds of Irishmen were serving with the British Forces. Smyllie called this, 'Cruel to the relatives.'

One night a news item which appeared in the rival Dublin dailies — the *Irish Independent* and the *Irish Press* — was deleted from the *Irish Times* proofs. "I'm going to put them to the test," Smyllie declared.

As it happened, the censors had just 'killed' on one of our proofs a review of a book referring to the duties of the ATS, the British women's service organization. R.M. waited for one week, then printed the same review — but this time he substituted the name of a German women's war organization for that of the ATS, a German name for the author's and a Berlin publishing firm for that of the London publishers.

The censors passed it this time! Smyllie got the two reviews printed on leaflets side by side. The first was headed KILLED BY CENSOR and the second, the German one, was headed PASSED BY CENSOR. These leaflets created a great sensation. R.M. had them distributed widely and even got a number smuggled out to other countries.

His telephone arguments with the Castle officials went on and once when he heard that they had been temporarily reinforced by civil servants from the Department of Agriculture he exclaimed: "You and your crowd of turnip-snodders are ruining our stories."

Aiken at one stage threatened that if Smyllie and his staff did not co-operate more fully an 'order' would be served requiring proofs to be submitted in page form rather than column by column. This threat if it had been carried out, could have been crippling. As it was, the censors became more strict, proofs came back slowly from the office of the Censorship at Dublin Castle, the paper was often late in 'getting away', and some trains were missed.

Sub-editors were kept busy rewriting blue-pencilled headlines and 'intros'. Often when pages had been made up at the 'stone' they had to be ripped apart again for further cuts. Then the officials began giving instructions about the size of headlines on battle reports, the length of stories, even where they should be placed in the page.

Proofs came back from the Castle bearing instructions: 'This report must not go at the top of a column. It must be printed down the page beneath the fold of the paper' . . . 'This headline must not be double-column — not more than single column' . . . 'This report must not appear in bold panel form, but as an ordinary news item in light type.'

The censors on occasion deleted mention of Sir John Maffey, British Representative in the Republic. They would not allow any photograph of him to be published. The *Irish Times* for generations had run a Court and Society column. Now the censors banned the word 'Court'. The name 'Kingstown' was struck out and was substituted by the Irish name. For example 'Kingstown Presbyterian Church' — its legal name — was altered to — 'Dun Laoghaire Presbyterian Church'. The title 'Forces Programme' was deleted from the BBC list in the radio column.

Death notices of serving Irishmen were censored. Their rank and regiment or unit and place of death were struck out. Smyllie refused to allow some death notices to be published as altered. This blue-pencilling of death notices caused annoyance to grieving relatives as the war continued. Phrases like 'Greater love hath no man' were deleted.

The following are other examples of the censorship.

A proof of a leading article by Smyllie referring to mass demonstrations in St Peter's Square, Vatican City — returned by censor marked *'This article deleted in its entirety.'*

Story headed 'Mussolini's downfall' . . . altered to *'Signor Mussolini's resignation'.*

An eight-column streamer headline for the front page 'Allied tanks in Catania suburbs' — the censor's blue-pencilled instructions on the proof said *'Passed subject to restriction of heading to four columns'.*

Censors gave an order that no heading on the fighting in Italy was to be 'too big.'

'Allied aircraft pounded Sicily' — altered to *'attacked Sicily'.*

'Allies now have air superiority over Southern Italy' — killed by censor.

'Great pillars of smoke from burned houses and villages pinpoint the Germans' path as they withdraw northwards in Italy. Villagers have been shot, cattle destroyed, and rail tracks torn up' — killed.

'Wave upon wave of American planes flew over the Italian capital' — killed.

'Photographs taken reveal accuracy of bombing of Rome' — killed.

'Pope's plea for peace' — double-column heading killed.

'Anti-German demonstrations in Milan' — killed.

'Vatican City under protection of Germans' — killed.

A report of a broadcast message to Italy by the former Mayor la Guardia of New York was returned by the censor marked 'Deleted in its entirety'. (La Guardia wanted to see Italy throw in its lot with the Allies.)

Officials dealt severely with reports from Soviet sources about the fighting. In general they killed comments by Russian military spokesmen, extracts from Moscow newspapers, and all items referring to celebrations over the recapture of cities from the Germans.

A proof of one of Smyllie's leading articles was returned marked: 'Deleted in its entirety' — the article contained such sentences as 'The German offensive proved to be a failure . . . the Red Army rolled it back'.

One news report from Reuters stated: 'Red Army forces are moving up along the whole front with clockwork precision'. The censors knocked out the words 'with clockwork precision.'

Other examples:

'The twilight of an army is setting in on the Dneiper bend' — killed.

'German prisoners admitted that the tank crews could not stand up to the terrific fire of the Soviet anti-tank guns' — killed.

'No army has ever carried out such a prolonged and continuous offensive as the Red Army' — killed.

'Evacuation of the Crimea by the Germans has already begun' — killed.

'Melitopol is becoming a huge graveyard of German dead' — killed.

'Reuters states that it is no risky forecast to say that the German cause at this stage is well-nigh hopeless' — killed.

This item referred to the great battle for Kiev and the censors also deleted the following descriptive passage: 'There is hardly one chance in a hundred that the Germans can do anything other than delay defeat. German troops fleeing in disorder for the river are trying to get across to the western bank on rafts, or by clinging to logs and empty barrels, or even to horses' tails. Many hundreds of bodies have been washed ashore on the low lying Dneiper island of Khoritsa.'

Another story which led to protest was the deletion of a dramatic broadcast by the BBC. For a time R.M. was so upset that he seemed to be in the mood to 'publish and be damned'. "Let them send me to prison," he declared. "It will be a big advertisement for the *Irish Times*."

There is no doubt that he would have been prepared to go to prison if things had come to a head. After all, he had been interned once before, briefly as a civilian in Germany.

The broadcast which caused the row followed a series of raids by British troops who landed on Crete and destroyed German war planes on airfields. In a 'special message' to the people of Crete the broadcast stated: 'This is not an invasion. The day is coming when the signal will be given for the warriors of Crete to fight side by side with invasion forces to exact justice for your enemy's crimes. Till then stay in your places. Avoid giving provocation to the enemy. Await your moment.'

Also killed were an important Allied message to Greece broadcast by the BBC; the headline 'RAF drop 1,000 tons of bombs on Cologne'; and stories referring to the illness or whereabouts of Hitler and Goering.

Smyllie's confrontations with the censorship became celebrated throughout Ireland, but apart from James Dillon, deputy leader of the Fine Gael party, R.M. received little support from politicians. Dillon, an eloquent Dail Deputy, wanted the country to reconsider its neutrality stance and to support the United States and Britain — without involving Irish troops. But his stance was rejected by de Valera and by most of his own party.

"Bigger Allied Air Offensive Coming

G........... Sir Archibald Sinclair, British Secretary for Air at a Constitutional Club luncheon in London yesterday, add-ing: ".................................

For many months to come," he said, "the process of expansion of both the British and American Bomber Commands will continue. The range and weight of their hammer blows will increase. The battle of the Ruhr will rank as one of the decisive battles of history. Make no doubt about it, these wounds will prove mortal."

German military power was rocking to its foundations, he said, as result of the offensive conducted with the support and co-operation of Fighter Command and the tactical air force by the British and American Bomber Commands.

People talked about a second front, but there was no front that the German people .... the German High Command feared more than the air front.

"Let the British .... over Germany by night and the Americans by day," continued Sir Archibald. "We did not gloat over the destruction of German cities, but half-measures were cruel in war, be-cause they prolonged the agony and wasted life.

"Germany has no longer any hope of winning the war. Only Hitler is prolonging it. The time will come when German people will be asking—'Why should we die for Hitler and the Nazis and the junkers?' Re-member, then, the men who fought the battle of the Ruhr, the battle of Hamburg, and the battle of Berlin. They have never failed us; we must not fail them."

O. SPARKS

BRUCE HOBBS GETS M.C.

Acting-Captain Bruce Hobbs, the steeplechase rider, who won the 1938 Grand National on Battleship, has been awarded the M.C. Bruce was only 17 when he won the Grand National. The same year his back was broken in a fall at Cheltenham and it was thought he would never ride again, but he made a remarkable recovery. He has been on service more than three years in the Middle East, where he has been twice wounded.

Threat of German Air Reprisals

Paques, the Paris radio commentator, said last night:—

"England is now faced with the menace of a German counter-air offensive. A newly-born Luftwaffe stands ready, manned by picked crews, filled with the desire to avenge thousands of dead. Militarily Germany has always kept her pro-mises. She may delay the dreadful hour of reprisals, but this hour will come.

"Calm and composed, Germany is keyed up for a blow which will astound the world, however hardened to blows it may be."—A.P.

BERLIN SAYS— "Hitler and Goering Not Ill"

Reports that Herr Hitler and Marshall Goering are ill were emphatically denied in political quarters in Berlin, quoted by Calais Radio last night.

"All reports concerning the Fuehrer are as completely false as previous reports of a similar nature," it was stated.

"Equally untrue are Stockholm reports that Reichmarshal Goering is ill, and that General Keitel has taken over."—(Reuter.)

A few examples of Censors' cuts — Irish Times wartime proofs.

A prisoner in Belfast Gaol who attended weekly classes conducted by the author produced this drawing of a local newspaper. He was 'in' for forgery!

Smiles all round as Cary Grant, ever the professional, advises the photographer on the angle from which to take the picture. With the film star are the author and wife, Mrs Dorothy Orr.　　　　　*(Photo: Associated Newspapers)*

Princess Margaret and Lord Snowdon, interviewed during a visit to the home of Lord and Lady de Vesci at Abbeyleix during the sixties. "We hope to be back in Ireland soon," the princess said then — but later the two were divorced.

(Photo: Charles Fennell)

The boy who became one of the richest men. Gerald Grosvenor, photographed with his sisters at Ely Lodge, Co. Fermanagh, when he was aged 7, told me he wanted to be "a taxi driver or maybe a soldier in the Foreign Legion." Today he is the Duke of Westminster and owner of an area of London.

(Photo: Associated Newspapers)

FIGHTING TALK! Archbishop Marcel Lefebvre, the so-called rebel prelate, tells the author in Switzerland of how he had been on the 'verge of 'coming to blows' with Pope Paul VI.
(Photo: Charles Fennell — reproduced by permission of News Group Newspapers)

"The headhitter's decision is final," says comic Ken Dodd at a newspapermen's Christmas dinner party. Seated next to him: J. L. Manning, well-known sports editor, and the author.   *(Photo: Associated Newspapers)*

The late R. M. ('Bertie') Smyllie — celebrated Editor of the Irish Times.
(Photo: Irish Times*)*

Author and wife Dorothy at a mid-sixties London Press Ball.

My mother, Margaret Orr — she overcame bitter blows.

DEATH CELL LETTER

This dramatic letter was written by George Kelly on the day before his execution at Liverpool Prison. Members of his family and friends maintained throughout that he had been wrongly convicted of murder. One of them said: 'He was framed. He swore his innocence before God just a few hours before he was to hang.' (See pp.91-92)

In replying to this letter, please write on the envelope

Number 7915 Name G. Kelly

Prison

I suppose you know that I have got to go in the morning, hard luck kid but it looks like I have just got to go this way, believe me it is very hard for me but the only thing that hurts my feelings is being innocent of this terrible crime

please look for

3

Well I had a letter today from she said she always talks to Mam, There is one thing I have got to tell you, If it is possible, when she goes to the I.O.M. I do hope she will try and come back and take Mother over there for a week it will do her good. Believe me its a smashing day, the sun is coming through my cell window, to think I have got to leave all that behind, it breaks my heart at times

Please look after Mother and Dad for me.

me, if you only knew how much I loved that girl, these wicked people have put me where I am to-day, they have parted me from my poor Mother and father and you, also my sweetheart.

I know you have done everything you can do

I only hope from the bottom of my heart, That you will try to find the man who done the Cameo Murder. Before God and the Blessed Virgin Mary, I will stand a innocent man, How is my girl, how is my darling tell her I love her a lot,

4

Well I do love you as a you are my best kid, its bad I have got to leave you. Well I promise you I will always pray for you. This is my last letter to you when you get this I will be gone into the next world. Sorry but I am afraid I will have to say Good Bye, and Good Luck to you, Look after Mam and Dad.

George

X X X

Chapter 16

'LEAKS' AND PHONE TAPS

Downing Street letter had to be read to Dev

Smyllie lived in Pembroke Park, in the Ballsbridge district of Dublin. The office gossip was that his domestic life — what there was of it — was strictly ruled by his wife Kathleen and their maid Margaret. Once when he was laid up with an attack of flu John Murdoch, a well-known reporter, called at his house with the generous gift of a packet of tea — which was scarce then. Murdoch liked to tell the story later — "The woman whoever it was snatched the tea from my hand and banged the door — never even said thanks. I hope he got the tea."

In the office one evening Smyllie disclosed that he had 'a first-class story' about telephone tapping and leakages of important information — but the story could not be published! "It would be killed by the censorship the moment the copy reached the Castle," he said. "I wouldn't even give them the satisfaction of reading it and then putting the blue pencil through it."

R.M. said he had learned that the reason de Valera was taking only leading officials of the Foreign Affairs Department into his confidence was that officials had alerted him about important 'classified' news being disclosed as a result of gossip.

The Editor, who had many informants, was satisfied his information was from a trustworthy source, and he told us: "The Long Fella is now more careful than ever about whom he takes into his confidence. Some of his recent remarks to Cabinet colleagues about neutrality and his attitude towards Britain and the United States have been repeated outside Government Buildings.

"The story is that the secret service have discovered that a few officials as well as the wives of certain Government Ministers have been gossiping. Official permission was given to place a 'tap' on their telephones and on the phones of other unnamed persons. One of the subjects leaked referred to joint discussions between highly placed officers of the Irish and British forces in the Border area."

On this and other occasions Smyllie mentioned that his own phone was being tapped. "I don't care what they hear me saying," he said. "They

73

74

know what I think about things in any case. But I wouldn't like anyone else to get into trouble. When a good friend rings me I often begin by saying, 'You realize that our friends are listening in to this phone'."

* * *

Mr de Valera at this time was taking tremendous responsibility on his own shoulders. As well as being head of the Government, he had complete charge of foreign affairs — a duty from which there was no respite. Day after day he was dealing with problems affecting neutrality, food scarcity, IRA activities, and approaches from Washington, London and Berlin. Some of these approaches he must have regarded as barely concealed threats. His dilemma then was aggravated by the fact that he was almost blind at times. But reports about his eyesight trouble and visits from specialists were not published. The eye trouble had first affected him just after his 20-year-old son Brian was killed in a riding accident in Phoenix Park.

His sight deteriorated so greatly that once when Sir John Maffey visited him with a personal letter from the former British Prime Minister Neville Chamberlain he could not read it properly. Maffey had to take it back and read it out to him! Most people were unaware that the country's destinies at a fateful stage later were in the sole care of a leader who at times could not see properly to read a letter. His sight improved subsequently after an operation.

But what would have happened if at a certain period de Valera had gone completely and permanently blind — or if his death had occurred? With a different leader could circumstances have arisen in which an invasion might have taken place and Ireland could have become a battlefield?

Frank Aiken had been Dev's 'comrade in arms' for many years, yet at critical moments the leader invariably consulted with his main advisers in the Department of External Affairs, Joseph Walshe, secretary, and Frederick Boland (who later became a United Nations General Assembly President).

Aiken had ambitions to be Minister for External Affairs, but it was not until after the General Election of 1951 that Dev allowed the vital portfolio to go to him. He may have been partly influenced by controversy and intrigue surrounding Aiken's 1941 mission to the United States to defend neutrality and to ask President Roosevelt for ships, arms and supplies. Aiken during that trip encountered opposition from some US politicians.

Dev loyally defended his colleague against all criticisms at the time and Gray, the American Minister in Dublin, was felt in some quarters to have schemed against Aiken's mission. The US Ambassador in London then, Joseph P. Kennedy, was not entirely trusted by London and Washington, and after the Tyler Kent affair diplomatic messages between Britain and the US were re-routed. Tyler Kent was a cipher clerk in the American Embassy in whose London apartment 'top secret' messages were discovered — the contents of which had been transmitted to Hitler.

* *

"There are more Christians attending churches in Russia today than there are church-goers in the whole of the British Isles" — a spokesman interviewed during a visit to Soviet Russia.

* *

Smyllie, with his own informative contacts, said one evening during discussion on the night's splash: "The best story, if we could print it, would be what went on when Roosevelt received Aiken. The version I've been hearing is that Roosevelt lost his temper, attacked Frank over his attitude, and virtually showed him the door."

Although opposing de Valera's presidential style of Government Smyllie had a personal regard for him and never doubted his integrity. This was illustrated during the dramatic general election campaign of May-June 1944 which seemed at times more like a fight between Smyllie and the *Irish Times* on one side and de Valera and Aiken on the other.

R.M. advocated the setting up of a National Government as a 'progressive and unifying step' with Dev as its head. The *Irish Times* and a row over an American Note about the Axis diplomats in Dublin figured prominently in that election campaign. It was a remarkable episode — a strong Prime Minister engaged in a daily wordy duel with an editor when at any moment both they and their small state could have been swamped and crushed by great warring powers.

Happy in a dogfight of this kind the Editor prowled round his office each night devouring every item of election news and suddenly bursting into one of his ribald songs. When the election was over the irony of the situation struck him and he exclaimed: "The gods must be laughing at the antics of we mortals. The Long Fella has won the General Election — and the other news is that the Second Front has just been opened!"

The antagonism between Smyllie and Aiken flared openly after a Dail speech by Aiken. The Minister declared, "Those at the *Irish Times* have a different outlook on many things from that of the vast majority of the Irish people."

R.M. growled, " I'm not letting him get away with an unscrupulous gibe like that," and in a leading article next night he wrote: 'It is because we differ — and we differ honestly — from the Minister that he now has drawn in public that dagger that has been wielded so dexterously in private during the last few years . . . we are convinced that in his attitude the Minister is exceeding his legal powers . . . we leave him to the mercy of his own forensic style.'

Aubrey Viggars, Northern Editor of the Sunday Dispatch. *He later joined the staff of the* Daily Telegraph.

Chapter 17

NO APOLOGIES

'Castle was forced to keep a keen eye on me'

The eventual collapse of German resistance had little effect on the censorship. Many first-class stories by some of the best war correspondents about the last hours of the Third Reich were 'killed'. But two items *were* passed without alteration — the death of Hitler by his own hand in his bunker on 30 April, 1945, and three days later the fact that Prime Minister de Valera called on Dr Hempel, German Minister in Dublin to express 'condolence'. Smyllie commented: "Some of Dev's colleagues urged him against going to Hempel with his sympathy. If he insisted he should have done it privately and not shame the whole country."

When news of Germany's final defeat was officially announced students of Trinity College, Dublin — founded by Queen Elizabeth in 1591 — held a victory demonstration and hoisted the Union Jack and other Allied flags. This resulted in counter demonstrations. Windows in the *Irish Times* and other buildings were smashed by stone-throwers. Police made baton charges. The gates of TCD had to be locked and students confined to their quarters.

Smyllie was not perturbed. "The stone-throwers are really paying us a compliment," he said. "Our stand has been justified. If the Germans had won the war stone-throwers would be thrown into some prison camp."

The censorship was lifted on 11 May, 1945, and next morning the *Irish Times* let itself go in a denunciation. 'We have been living and speaking in conditions of unspeakable humiliation' the leading article declared.

It expressed resentment that the paper had been 'singled out' for specially severe treatment — the only newspaper forced to submit to the censorship in advance 'every inch' of printed matter — including even the small advertisements.

Smyllie had admittedly made the censorship look ridiculous on occasion by referring to 'boating accidents' and 'lead poisoning incidents — and as time passed many readers grew to appreciate the intensity of the contest that was going on between Westmoreland Stree and the Castle.

"I am, and always have been, strongly pro-British," he said later. "If the same or a similar situation were to arise tomorrow I should act in precisely the same way as I acted throughout the war. I have no apologies to make to anybody.

"The censorship was often stupid and irritatingly inept. But the fact that the *Irish Times* was avowedly, and I might also say aggressively pro-British put the censorship in an awkward position. It was forced to keep a closer eye on the *Irish Times* than normally might have been necessary. It smashed and hacked at our copy in order to make sure that nobody was putting a quick one over Dublin Castle.

"They prevented me from open support of the Allies, often going to preposterous lengths in the process. But they were meticulous in their efforts to be neutral. Their lapses were due to inexperience and over-anxiety rather than to malice."

In the years that followed much of the zest went out of Smyllie's life. He had little time for conferences with departmental managers or advertising men — apart from his faithful companion 'Pussy' O'Mahony.

He would often crumple up memos, throw them into the waste-paper basket, and march out to the pub. He became vastly overweight and with increasing illness had to retire. He died in 1954. It was 'the end of an era' people said. He had been an outstanding personality and no editor can have had such a massive funeral.

*   *   *

Smyllie was succeeded by his long-time deputy and loyal friend Alec Newman, the classical scholar turned journalist, who had shared with him so many turbulent events. But things later went wrong for Alec — largely because of his own conduct. He became an increasingly heavy drinker, and his language and behaviour were, at times eloquent.

Normally courteous, this gifted chap's conduct and his habit of telling people to 'kiss my arse' became so talked about that he was eventually summoned before the board of directors and resigned his job — the little cask of whiskey he kept concealed in his office was of no help when the crunch came. I happened to be in the editorial department of the *Evening Mail* — a sister paper of the *Irish Times* — at that moment and saw Newman as he emerged, white-faced and shaken. "The bastards have got me," he exclaimed, "and no 'handshake' after thirty-one years with the paper."

After that, Alan Montgomery became Editor of the *Irish Times*. Things might have been very different if Montgomery, a first class newspaperman, had only been made Editor on Smyllie's retirement. But Newman by unwritten law had traditional right of succession — regardless of the misgivings felt in several quarters.

Montgomery himself caused a stir after a comparatively short time by resigning in order to go to a more highly paid job as director of information at Guinness's Brewery! Douglas Gageby then took over, and the *Irish Times*, whose future had looked shaky in earlier years, began to progress. Gageby, at one time editor-in-chief of the short-lived Irish News Agency, had achieved great success with the newly-launched *Evening Press* and went to the *Irish Times* as managing editor and director.

Leaving the paper after about 26 years must have been a wrench for Alan Montgomery for whom so many well-known newsmen had worked — Tony Gray, later a successful author; Cathal O'Shannon, Tony Kelly, the late John Ross, Tom McCaughren, RTE security correspondent; Michael McInerney, Alan Bestic, Wesley Boyd, head of news at RTE — and notable photographers such as George Leitch and Dermot Barry.

Leitch had a reputation as a prankster, setting up absurd situations and on occasion sending staffmen off on wild-goose chases. But the joke was on him once when he talked Smyllie into allowing him to hire an aircraft to cover a Grand National at Aintree. George made the flight, went to town with his camera, flew back to Dublin — "Great trip, great pictures," he exulted. But a short while later he came down from the dark room. He wasn't grinning now. "A slight problem," he groaned. "Forgot to load the bloody camera!"

Could happen to anyone perhaps. George nevertheless was a brilliant photographer who got many remarkable pictures for the paper. Some of them, such as the dead babies clasped in each other's arms — victims of the 1941 German bombs on Dublin's North Strand — were not published at the time because of censorship.

I had enjoyed my years with the *Irish Times* and before I decided to leave Ireland for London Smyllie had roused himself sufficiently to ask, "Is it the money? Are you frustrated? You can be a big fish in a smaller pond in due course." What I wanted was the great wide world of newspaper life and work. I said goodbye to many friends — not least in the composing-room and machine departments — Joe Bolger, Barney

O'Rourke and the rest. The men in those departments had once got me to draw up a letter to management requesting a wage increase, and I was almost as pleased as they were when it was successful, and still recall the time-honoured and noisy 'knock-down' in the composing-room on the farewell night.

Chapter 18

FLEET STREET

Wife who kept phoning the news desk

And so — to Fleet Street — the Street of Adventure and all that, my big ambition, to work in the heart of newspaperland, realized. In fact I had already worked there as 'relief' for brief but eventful periods in wartime, the most memorable being during the blitz on the night of 29 December 1940 — the second 'Great Fire of London'.

St Bride's — the lovely Christopher Wren church, also known as the newspapermen's church — was one of the innumerable buildings fire-bombed that night. A crowd of us including Hughie Stalker the night news editor, rushed in from the PA and succeeded in saving the heavy lectern and some other church furnishings from the flames. We carried them into the basement of the Press Association-Reuters offices next door. There as the city burned we held a make-believe 'service'.

Charlie Jervis, a well-known PA staffman, standing at the lectern began: "Dearly beloved brethren, the Scripture moveth us in sundry places . . . " But then the great building suddenly shuddered — and we waited for the annihilating explosion. After a time we ventured out into Fleet Street. There we found a huge torpedo-like bomb, with heavy parachutes attached, lying in the middle of the road.

"Adolf forgot to wind it up," joked Harry Turner, another PA man, and as the blitz continued we danced around, hopping to and fro over the 20ft 'monster' and singing "Run rabbit, run."

Sounds crazy now — but London was burning all around that night, right up to St Paul's Cathedral and it was a mad world then and for many other nights of that grim and deadly winter.

My first staff jobs in London were with the two great agencies, first the Press Association and then Reuters. A bedlam of chaos was one's first impression of these where later one of the 'copy boys' was an East End kid named Derek Jameson — whom, years later, I was to serve under when he became one of Murdoch's editors — and later still, he became a television and radio 'star' and was honoured with an award by the Variety Club.

It wasn't chaos, of course, when one got the hang of things in those non-stop, round-the-clock 'news factories'. There's always a newspaper edition about to 'roll' somewhere and the agencies' job is to keep the taps at full 'on' with the flow of news. One of my early recollections: Frank Turner — he was the PA night editor — peering briefly over my shoulder at my shorthand notes and exclaiming "Oi, oi — is there a 'snap' in it?" What he meant was: did the story on which I was working merit the sending of a brief 'snap' message over the DP (the direct-printer service then in use) warning newspaper offices that an important report was on the way — for example: 'Rush — apartment block fire — 15 feared dead'.

My first reaction was of wonderment — how the heck could Frank so quickly and from a distance read another chap's shorthand notes — each person having his own peculiar style, and mine being peculiarly peculiar. But then Frank was a remarkable character in many ways — always a couple of jumps ahead of everyone else.

Another memorable 'live wire' night editor of the PA Walton Cole, a Scotsman, strode unendingly, tirelessly and perspiringly round the office — like a tiger in search of prey: in his case a big story hiding in there behind some harmless-looking paragraph. To someone hesitating over a story he urged, "Get on with it — be bold," and then hurried off. A brilliant news man — but, sadly, he died at an early age, a severe loss to Fleet Street.

At first in London I stayed in a large 'residential club' in the Gray's Inn Road district — but quickly grew to dislike the place. In reality it was a warren of small dark rooms and dismal corridors. Returning to it and its equally depressing inhabitants was like going into prison. Residential club! A grim joke. After that I got a pleasant 'pad' in Montague Street, Bloomsbury. Not only was it within easy reach of Fleet Street but it had a kindly landlady Delia, who seemed to divine when you'd had a rough night and sent up breakfast, bless her.

After only about ten days at the PA I was stunned to be told, "You have the weekend off, old boy!" I had put in some overtime and this combined with a Friday and a Sunday constituted a weekend — a novelty to me and a tribute to the PA duty rostering system. With this unexpected leave I decided to pay my mother a surprise visit and caught the Liverpool boat. But when I walked in to greet her she exclaimed, "Heavens, have you given up that job then?" When she heard that I'd been given the weekend off she commented, "Delightful — you never got that in all the years you were working here."

Dead right she was — one unpredictable day off in a fortnight, if lucky.

The snag about working on news agencies is that after all one's efforts there's no newspaper! One's work is flashed into others offices in London and the provinces. As Hugo Manning, a popular Reuters colleague, said "One misses the end product — the thrill of watching YOUR newspaper pouring down off the machines."

So eventually it was 'Goodbye, agencies' — and back to newspapers, in Fleet Street and Manchester. Back, too, to the camaraderie and friendships of newspapermen — the larger-than-life characters, the good, the bad and the ugly, the decent blokes — and the creeps who run to the boss with ideas, other people's ideas. And the fellows who didn't make it. The tormented colleague who threw himself to death from a window. The one suffering from nerves who died under a train. Another, found gassed. Still another, at the foot of a cliff. Many — who went under prematurely from nervous and mental breakdowns, heart attacks and, of course, booze.

* *

"I once worked on a newspaper, briefly, as a reporter. Then the editor and I agreed that my talents would enable me to do better at something else"
— actor Peter O'Toole during an interview.

* *

I worked on daily papers, then on 'evenings' and later on Sunday papers — by turns sub-editing, reporting, feature writing. The papers included the *Daily Mail, Sunday Dispatch,* the *Evening Mail,* the *Sunday Review* and *News of the World* and was successively chief reporter, features editor, assistant editor, and deputy editor.

* * *

The goings-on in some Fleet Street offices were as choice as the stories being written up. In one there was a much gossiped-about affair between the news editor and the wife of the night editor. The wife, often seen in bars near the office, was in the habit of phoning the news desk regularly to arrange meetings. The night editor, a dour type, suspected that his wife was playing around and made calls to his home each evening. Whether he realized that the news editor was involved with her was not clear but he often looked over at the news desk during calls, and his expression was not cordial.

One evening after the news editor had put down the phone, spoken to his deputy and then left the office, the night editor, a few moments later, got up abruptly from his chair and strode out of the room. This was unheard of at that busy time — he invariably took a 'break' more than an hour later. Mutters of "Trouble brewing" and "Dirty work at the cross roads tonight" from subordinates.

About three-quarters of an hour afterwards, the night editor returned to his desk, pale and shaken. But the news editor did not return that night or during the next two weeks. We learned later that the night editor had made a round of the bars, discovered his wife with the other chap, gone berserk, attacked and injured both of them. The news editor, suffering from cuts, took an early holiday — and another job. The wife and her husband split up — she moved away and was not heard of again at the office.

In another newsroom, Tony, a rugged good-looking fellow in his mid-thirties, was from Scotland but had spent much of his newspaper career abroad. Now he was 'back in civilization' as he said, and intent on having a good time. He was good company and a great talker. His charm and chat made a hit with the girls in the office.

Despite his easy-going conversation he never gave much information about himself. "Old Tony's been here for months now, and seems a great guy, but we still know damn all about him," remarked Peter, the copy-taster, one evening. "Maybe there's a wife and kids somewhere in the background."

In that office the management had constructed a number of bedrooms on the top floor to accommodate editorial staffmen working on late-running stories who might miss their last trains. Tony, a late bird socially, made more use of the top floor than the rest of the staff combined. It also transpired that he was making more use of the facility than the management had in mind.

One morning, in the early hours with only a few late staff still on duty Tony, in pyjamas and dressing-gown, rushed into the news-room. This wasn't the usual self-possessed Tony. He was agitated and dishevelled.

"You've got to help me," he exclaimed. "It's Betty. She's up there. She's unconscious. For God's sake . . . . " He was trembling.

Betty was a secretary-typist in the office. It was known that Tony had been paying her a lot of attention. Three of us — the entire staff there at that hour — rushed upstairs with him. One colleague had the presence of mind to get a noggin bottle of brandy he had in his locker. Betty, in her nightie, was lying sprawled on the bed in Tony's room. She was unconscious. Her face was deathly pale, her long blonde hair, usually so neat, now in disarray.

Bill, the 'late man' on the news desk, took immediate charge. "Open the windows, wide," he directed. "Get me a sponge and some cold water. You — phone for an ambulance, just in case." Then he opened the bedroom door. "It'll create a draught, the fresh air will help," he said.

He sponged the girl's face and neck repeatedly with the cold water. From a shelf he took some bath-salts and held them to her nose — "Should serve as smelling salts," he muttered. To our tremendous relief Betty stirred and moaned slightly. Bill bent down and called, "Betty, Betty. Come on Betty, wake up." She stirred again, but not until she had opened her eyes a few moments later did Bill reach for the brandy — a little of which he gave to her using a teaspoon. She was in a very weak state but after a while was able to get up and take some hot coffee. Later on at her insistence we got a taxi and she was driven home.

She never returned to that office and we heard she had taken another job.

What happened earlier in the bedroom on the top floor that night never became known. Tony, who had always been so chatty, now became the quiet man. Then he vanished, as suddenly as he had arrived. There were stories that the management had received enquiries about him from private investigation agencies. Peter commented: "They were both lucky that night. They were obviously messing with drugs. She could have snuffed it if Bill hadn't been so quick — and then friend Tony would have been in a nasty situation."

*   *   *

They were an extremely varied lot, all those 30 or more editors whom I encountered during the years. Those whom I regarded as the finest were Willie Armour, R.M. Smyllie, Charles Eade, Aubrey Viggars, Herbert Gunn, Bill Hardcastle, Eldred Reeve and Stafford Somerfield — all first-class newspapermen, fearless, straightforward and without pretence or pomposity. They were the sort of men who were not afraid to ignore 'advice' or hints from on high when they thought fit.

Some other editors lacked their strength of character and purpose — such as the man who spent too much of his time in posh hotel bars, and when he was full of drink and vanity harangued customers and barmen alike with scurrilous remarks concerning the proprietors and management. Then, leaning over the bar counter, he poured his glass of brandy down the basin and exclaimed, "That's what I think of the . . . . paper."

This repeated idiotic and astounding behaviour eventually led to his downfall — which was sudden and dramatic. When he strolled into his office one morning, somewhat late, as was his custom, he was confronted by a stony-faced Chairman who was waiting for him. After a few sharp and devastating words he was handed a cheque by the Chairman, and was drummed out of the building without having the chance to take off his coat.

Certain persons, I think, find themselves in the editorial chair not because of any great merit but because of the 'next-in-line' syndrome — and indeed in some instances because they are no good at anything else. In my experience quite a number had been useless either as reporters, sub-editors, lay-out men or even caption writers. In fact, some could be described as a hindrance — no joking! One of these who comes immediately to mind was untidy and unorganized in every respect. He roamed about the office, picking up stories, carrying them from one desk to another, gossiping to subs and reporters, then setting down the half-read copy far from where it should have been — blithely oblivious to the delays and confusion he caused.

As for the photographs constantly pouring in for consideration he placed them in heaps on a big table and allowed them to mount up each day. Soon there was a 'mountain' of unwanted pictures. His custom was to pick out photos from the middle of the pile, give a whistle of surprise and declare, "We'll use these — marvellous." When someone remarked, "Those were in the Daily So-and-so last Monday," he just grinned and remarked, "Not to worry, they're not readers of our paper." After choosing a picture of someone in the news he usually seized a ruler and drew cut-lines closely around the person's eyes and nose — so that when the photo eventually appeared in the paper it was grotesque and virtually unrecognizable.

It's odd how some people change completely — when they are promoted, for example. Promotions sometimes have the opposite effects to those intended. Instead of improving things they may make them much worse. And the persons moved up don't in the long run always benefit.

One renowned and first-class news editor who was promoted to be associate editor 'changed' remarkably in almost every respect. He became a martinet disliked by everyone, began to lead a 'double life', fell foul of his editor-in-chief and senior colleagues, was eventually dismissed after a showdown, walked out of the office with a large 'golden handshake' — and disappeared completely for more than a year amid a spate of rumours and speculation.

This man when news editor could scent a good story and drove his men into the ground to get a scoop — and they respected him. But after his promotion he became aloof, touchy and abrupt. His mood was often sarcastic and even former colleagues found him unapproachable — "He's become a right nasty bastard," was perhaps the kindest remark made about him.

On Friday nights just before pub closing time he had the custom of rising suddenly and stalking out of the office without a word. The story spread that after drinking at a club with some 'old mate' he usually left town and went off to spend the weekend hill climbing. There was a noticeable relaxation of tension after he left the editorial department in this way. Jokes swept the office — "How would you like to spend your holiday hill climbing with The Man — or would you rather spend it in Siberia?"

One Friday night a news-room colleague who had been peering from the door of his office to make sure The Man had really departed beckoned: "I've discovered what he really gets up to at the weekends. You can forget all the yarns about hill climbing. The only climbing he does is with a certain young woman not a hell of a long way from this office — in her flat."

He mentioned one of the secretaries in the office. Another thing: "I hear the knives are out for him. He's been slashing and spiking expenses of some old retainers and the management are livid."

He was right. Soon afterwards there was a showdown and the man who had once been such a great news editor now found himself out on the street with his big pay-off. Fleet Street was full of rumours when in the midst of all the gossip he disappeared. The favoured view was that he had gone to Australia with the secretary.

Then about eighteen months later, suddenly, there he was, outside the Old Bell. "Hello, old boy, how's things?" he said casually. Not a word about himself, or about newspapers, which had been his whole life. He looked ill. Later a colleague, telling of his death, suggested that his unyielding nature prevented him asking anyone to give him a job.

Chapter 19

MURDER DRAMAS

Death sentence panic of innocent Alf

Newspapermen being a gregarious and thirsty lot it's perhaps not surprising that many staff changes and appointments originate in the fructifying atmosphere of the pub. And so it was in my own case — a chat at the Cheshire Cheese, in Fleet Street, heralded a move to Associated Newspapers — the *Daily Mail* and its sister paper the *Sunday Dispatch*, whose 'descendant' today, in tabloid form, is the *Mail on Sunday*. In fact the move was, in a way, like rejoining old friends because earlier, in Ireland, I had done stories for both papers to assist John Parker, mentioned previously.

While working for the *Sunday Dispatch* I got involved in an exciting episode with a man who figured in a sensational double murder trial. He was Alfred Merrifield, who with his wife Louie appeared in the dock at Manchester Assizes, both accused of the murder of Mrs Sarah Ann Ricketts, an elderly widow, in her bungalow at Blackpool.

The trial, which continued for eleven days, intrigued millions because of its mystery — who slipped poison into the coffee of the kindly woman who had befriended Alfred and Louie by taking them to live in her home? Mrs Ricketts had been widowed twice. Each husband was found gassed in the kitchen. Small wonder the place was called 'the bungalow of death'.

Alfred, a good-humoured dapper character who always carried a silver-knobbed walking stick, got along well with Sarah and helped her with jobs around the house and garden. She gave him a gold watch, then a diamond ring and other gifts. But Louie, who drank a lot, quarrelled with Sarah and nagged at the old lady to sign over the bungalow.

The trial of the Merrifields was full of drama. Day after day Louie sat motionless in the dock, her hard dark eyes fixed balefully on each witness. But Alfred, who was partially deaf, could not grasp what was going on. At one stage he broke down in frustration, waved his hands at the judge, and cried out, "Let me go below. You can finish it here. I can't hear what they're saying."

Louie was found guilty, but the jury disagreed about Alfred. As the judge put on the black cap to sentence Louie to death Alfred stood staring with horror. Not being able to hear properly he thought that he, too, was going to the scaffold. Of many strange court scenes I have watched, that was the most dramatic.

As he was being led below, I got close to the rails of the dock, gave him a thumbs-up sign, and told him, "You are OK." He smiled, for the first time in the long trial. He knew me well because I had visited him in Strangeways Prison with gifts of tobacco, and he had written to me several times. Back in gaol awaiting a new trial Alfred, still carrying his silver-knobbed stick, declared: "I have no fears, I am innocent."

Suddenly, a few days later the prison governor announced that the case against him had been dropped and he was free — 'without a stain on his name.' Scores of newspapermen and camera men besieged Strangeways to get his own story of the 'bungalow of death'. But there was no sign of Alfred.

Recalling that he had told me of the gold watch and other possessions which he had left in the bungalow I took a chance and drove straight to Blackpool. Luck was in for, on arrival, there was Alfred just getting out of a police car. He had been smuggled out through a side door of the gaol.

Police cordoned off the bungalow to keep reporters and crowds of sightseers away from him. I scribbled a few words addressed to Alfred on a page of my notebook and got a police officer I knew to deliver it. Alfred had now entered the house and in a few minutes the officer signalled me. As I nipped in there was a rush by others to follow but I managed to get the front door shut and chained.

I found Alfred marooned in the tiny vestibule unable to get into the living-room whose door had been locked while he was in gaol. Other newsmen were now hammering on the front door. One pushed a note through the letter-box saying, 'You must need a drink. I've got a bottle of Scotch here. Open the door.' Another called out, "The Press Council will hear about this. Open the door." Daftest remark of the week!

Eventually Alfred and I got the living-room door opened and the first thing he did was to look for the gold watch and the diamond ring. "They've been taken," he cried angrily. Nor could he find the keys of a safe which he said Mrs Ricketts had given him. He lit the gas-stove and put on the kettle to make tea.

Crowds were milling outside the bungalow. Suddenly we saw groups climbing over the wall behind the house. Alfred rushed out and hit some of them with his stick. Then he grabbed the kettle, rushed out shouting, "You bastards," and swung streams of the now boiling water at them. The invaders vanished in seconds.

A colleague of mine Dennis Johnson then called through the letter-box. He had a taxi waiting. Opening the front door suddenly Alfred and I, arms linked, made a dash for the cab. The crowd closed on us but Alfred laid about him with that stick. Unfortunately as we got near the cab he stumbled and almost fell into a hole in the footpath where repair men had been working. Recovering, we piled into the taxi and shouted, "Drive like hell towards Manchester. Special fee for you."

The cabbie was great. The taxi swayed wildly as we tried to shake off about thirty cars revving madly in our wake. Passers-by stopped to stare at the furious cavalcade which swept through the famous resort. In the back Alfred rolled on the floor, still hanging on to his stick. His natty Homburg which he usually wore at a sharp angle was over his eyes. But he was shouting like a schoolboy in delight: "Did you see me clout those fellows at the bungalow?" Strange to think that only a few hours previously he had been No. 1834 in Strangeways facing a murder charge.

A little way outside Blackpool we got clear of our pursuers, mainly through the skill and daring of our driver who at speed overtook a long string of coaches on a bend. Against oncoming traffic we were almost afraid to look. A big risk, but it paid off for us. The cars behind didn't chance it.

After about 15 miles we turned off the main road and had a meal in a secluded hotel until we felt that the heat was off. As darkness fell we continued our journey. But we had a narrow squeak when we suddenly found that we were driving just behind one of the cars still searching for us. We took a circuitous route and stayed overnight in Shrewsbury. Even in a hotel there we could not relax. Alfred, who talked rather loudly, would say, "The prison governor said to me, Mr Merrifield . . . . " and so on. Dennis and I had to shush him constantly. As he relaxed he told of the frustration he felt during his trial — "My life was being nattered away, and in the dock I couldn't hear anything properly. I broke down at times and wept in sheer helplessness."

And of his sudden release — "On my way out of Strangeways I passed a door leading to the scaffold. A shudder went through me. It could have been me, an innocent man going through that door."

We moved to a new hotel each day until the story MY TEN WEEKS IN THE SHADOW OF THE GALLOWS — ALFRED MERRIFIELD'S OWN STORY was safely in the paper.

Louie Merrifield did go to the scaffold — one of the last women to suffer the death penalty in England. (Ruth Ellis was the last.)

Alfred returned to Blackpool to live. But later he had to move out of the 'bungalow of death'. He lived subsequently in a caravan and died in his mid-sixties. The silver-knobbed stick, his faithful companion, was buried along with him.

In the course of the letters he sent me while he was in Strangeways Prison Alfred wrote:

'What an experience I've had to suffer, well knowing that I am perfectly innocent of any act or collaboration, or knowing of any act on the part of Mrs Merrifield against the old lady's death . . . I can assure you confidently that it is only a matter of time before I shall step out of here a free man to face the world without a stain on my mind. It will be a great relief when it is all over . . . . It is nothing but a damned rotten and foul charge from that big bully from Scotland Yard. May the Lord have mercy on his rotten mind.'

* * *

'It's a smashing day. The sun is coming through my cell window. To think I have to leave all that behind — it breaks my heart . . . When you get this I will be gone into the next world . . . '

This was part of the last letter written by George Kelly the day before he was hanged following the sensational Cameo Cinema murder trial in Liverpool. The letter, begged friends to look after his sweetheart — 'if you only knew how much I love that girl.'

Kelly, whose execution took place in March 1950, protested his innocence to the last and alleged that he was 'framed'. He wrote: 'I hope from the bottom of my heart that you will try to find the man who done the Cameo murder. Before God and the Blessed Virgin Mary I will stand an innocent man.'

Friends did their best to carry out his last wishes and repeatedly expressed their conviction that George had not murdered the cinema manager the previous year. In particular one friend, with whom I had a number of meetings, alleged that certain persons involved in the trial "Could not possibly have known George" and that George did not know them.

More than 20 years afterwards he told me: "I'm still searching deep for the truth — to bring to light the person or persons who really committed that murder. From the day I left the death cell in Walton Prison, having seen George for the last time, I have not left a stone unturned in my search — after all, how could a man swear his innocence before God just a few hours before he was to hang?"

*   *   *

The most baffling death mystery of all in my experience — one that has still never been solved — was the 'body on the beach' case. This affair, which became known as the 'riddle of the black panties girl', involved inquiries spreading from the West of Ireland to Dublin, London, Paris and across the Atlantic to New York and Miami. As the investigations went on the mystery grew ever deeper.

It all started one May morning in 1967 when a fisherman Martin O'Brien spotted a girl's body sprawled on lonely Doolin Strand, beneath the 668ft Cliffs of Moher. The body, with terrible injuries, was naked but for the black lace panties. As other persons became involved the case was to become one of the century's classic mysteries.

It took police 12 weeks to find out who the girl was — and then only by chance. She was 28-year-old Maria Domenech, a former beauty queen, of New York, known to her friends as 'Pinky'. She had become a social worker. The others mainly involved were her mother Mrs Virginia Domenech, 51, who vanished from her New York home within 10 days of Maria's death, and Patrick Darcy, 45, married, who was found dead in a Miami hotel bedroom as the mystery was at its height. He had been involved with both women.

One of the strangest episodes of this affair was a trip made to Paris and then Ireland by Maria and Darcy in that month of May. I discovered that the two had travelled on the same aircraft to Paris — but on different planes to Dublin via Heathrow on 22 May. Maria arrived in Dublin at 6 p.m. travelling under the name 'Miss Young'. Darcy, a travel agent, arrived five hours later under the name 'A. Young'. He was carrying ONE travel bag.

That night Darcy hired a self-drive car, checked in at a Shannon hotel at 8 a.m. on 23 May and left at midday. He returned the car to a Dublin hire firm the same evening. They said the gauge showed that he had travelled 700 miles. Driving direct to the hotel and back would have accounted for 260 miles. Where did he go to account for the remaining 440 miles? He flew alone from Dublin to Paris that night. He was carrying TWO travel bags.

But what of Maria 'Pinky' Domenech? What did she do during those 24 hours? Nobody knows that. The fisherman found her body at 9 a.m. on the beach on 24 May. A doctor said she had died as a result of a violent impact such as would result from falling from a great height and striking the ground feet first. In O'Brien's Tower, an ancient building on the sheer cliff top, below which the body was found, police discovered a scarf and a bloodstained bangle but no clothes.

Eight days after the finding of Maria's body her mother failed to turn up at the children's home in New York where she worked. Her apartment in Washington Heights was empty and Mrs Virginia Domenech has never been seen since. It was only after the mother was reported missing that it was discovered that Maria had also vanished — and it was Maria's fingerprints in a New York file which eventually led to her body being identified in Ireland.

Maria, the mysterious beauty, today lies buried in her native Puerto Rico, but many questions remain unanswered: what was the involvement between Patrick Darcy and Maria and her mother? Why did Darcy as I discovered visit Ireland at least six times before May, the month Maria died? Why were they using assumed names? What happened to 6,000 dollars Maria withdrew from a New York bank before she flew to Paris? Above all, did Patrick Darcy kill Maria? Did he kill her mother? And if so — why? When he was found dead in that hotel bedroom in Miami a few months after the others a bottle of whiskey lay near him — and outside his door hung a notice 'Do not disturb'.

*　　*　　*

Investigations during another murder case illustrated how easily a perfectly innocent person may become implicated. This story involved 'dating' agencies and secret meetings between a young man and a girl who later went missing and was eventually found strangled. The man, a university student, was questioned several times by police and later he told of the girl's visiting his apartment. His matter-of-fact attitude while being interviewed at a critical time was remarked upon by colleague Charles Sandell the Fleet Street crime reporter, and myself.

We had discovered that he was the son of a well-known peer but, while admitting this, he remained outwardly unperturbed. An unusual feature of this case was the activities of the dead girl's mother, who was busily conducting her own 'detective' investigations. Eventually, thanks to excellent police work, another young man, previously not mentioned, was tracked down and later tried, convicted and sentenced. But when it was all over one could not avoid the feeling that in different circumstances things could have gone terribly wrong for the student — his own aloof demeanour being no help to him at any stage.

*　　*　　*

When engaged on stories such as those just mentioned one was often reminded of the contrasts in people. Fairly businesslike in Britain — somewhat different from the 'Where are you from?' response in Ireland — persons approached there being more interested in finding out who YOU are! Harold Pendlebury, an outstanding *Daily Mail* reporter, used to remark, "Everything depends on how one approaches the person concerned — doesn't matter what country it is." True, although I've seen even Harold flummoxed in Wales. "The Welsh can be a little elusive," he admitted.

The most elusive character one could ever meet was a man nicknamed 'The Ringer'. I encountered him when working on a big smuggling story. It involved jewellery, industrial diamonds and gold leaf. He was recognized as the outstanding lone-wolf smuggler — and he may still be operating.

They nicknamed him 'The Ringer' because he could change his appearance almost instantly. Of average height he was nothing special to look at. Maybe that's where spies, too, are at an advantage. By being 'ordinary' looking, secret agents can melt into the background and not attract attention.

Anyway, 'The Ringer' was a better actor than many on the stage. He could play any part to disarm suspicion. Sometimes he would be a dapper young man, sometimes a brisk impatient business executive, sometimes an elderly man. By wearing glasses, combing his hair in different ways, adopting a limp or some other artifice he would become another person. Even his best friends couldn't recognize him for, in addition, he could alter his facial appearance. I had many friendly encounters with him and always he demonstrated his Pimpernel skill. Sometimes I have looked round trying to find him when he was only a few yards away from me, his appearance quite changed.

He specialized in smuggling top-grade stuff — platinum, gems, industrial diamonds. As well as being an artist in smuggling he was very independent. If advised to travel by a certain route he would be sure to go by different means. He would say in the racing language he used:

"Don't give me riding instructions. I know the course."

One day early in our acquaintance he said to me, "I will travel by the Belfast-Liverpool boat. I will arrive in Manchester by the first train. Bet you a score you don't recognize me." Foolishly, I suppose, I took on the £20 bet. I was at the station barrier for the first train and he did not pass me. I went to the café where we had arranged to meet. There he was laughing and saying, "You owe me." He had passed me all right. He told me in detail where I had been standing and other particulars. I checked on his departure and arrival times. There was no doubt.

He could get on a plane or boat with his stuff even if all the police and customs were specially watching for him. I've known him to be on a boat, have actually seen him on board, yet when I and my colleagues later went looking for him in every possible place, he just wasn't there.

Once he was on a cross-Channel vessel with a particularly heavy 'cargo' in his suitcases — and this time the Customs Officers somehow were 'on' to him. They introduced themselves while he was drinking a cup of coffee in the saloon. "Will you please come down as we wish to examine your luggage," they said. He went down. They examined his luggage. All he had was overnight clothes in a small case and a brief-case. The ship was delayed ten minutes in sailing that night before the Customs men retired, defeated. But the next day 'The Ringer' delivered his rich consignment at a Blackpool address. He was a bit nervy after this coup — but cool as ice while operating.

One day when he was travelling to England from the Continent an official glanced at his passport and then addressed him as 'Doctor'. The official had apparently been misled by an initial letter. The incident amused 'The Ringer' for a moment — then it suddenly gave him an idea — he used it to assume yet another identity.

The status of a doctor, he decided, would lend respectability and a certain dignity to him as a traveller. So in future, he often went about as 'Doctor'. He obtained a stethoscope and always had it prominently displayed on top of his things when his personal case was opened.

"I'll take the doctor," one Customs officer sometimes remarked to his colleague.

And 'The Ringer' prided himself that he looked the part. Once he gave an official who was dealing with him some advice on how to get rid of his troublesome cough.

*   *   *

Working on stories such as I have just described provided the opportunity, of course, to meet again old friends and contacts during Dublin visits. These included outstanding personalities like the late Paddy O'Hanrahan, formerly secretary to de Valera and later an aide to Prime Minister Charles Haughey, and the late Osmond Dowling, one of the country's best known journalists. At one period O'Hanrahan was head of the Government Information Bureau, as it was formerly called.

These two, along with some others, from time to time joined myself and colleagues such as Aubrey Viggars, Ronald Pearson (Chief reporter *Sunday Express*), Stafford Somerfield, Bill Taylor, George McIntosh or Phil Wrack for 'a glass of lunch' — events which on occasion had an alarming tendency to go on indefinitely.

The Senator — my old friend of former *Irish Times* days — was an entertaining and informative companion at some of these 'lunches' — but he had a surprise for me one day. "You won't see me here again," he said. "I'm leaving Dublin."

This was a shock for he loved the place and the life there. "Have to leave Dublin. My father died. Have to go back and look after things down the country."

I thought of my visit one time to his old home as his guest — his mother, old Aunt Juliet and her 'sundowners', his whiskey-drinking dad up in the attic gazing at the stars through his telescope. How would The Senator, who had become part of Dublin's social and pub life, settle down in such a different environment?

"This will be a severe blow to the licensees here."

"I'm the last of the Mohicans. It's up to me. There's no getting away from it. I have to go back. It's goodbye to all that."

A few pints, we wished each other luck — and cheerio. Some years afterwards I heard that he and Rosemary were married, with a family. So much for all his talk about remaining a 'free' man!

All's well that ends well — that was a saying of my jovial cousin Moore Mitchell, who also counselled 'There's always somebody trying to take the joy out of life!' In his case 'the somebodies' eventually succeeded because the prosperous business which he built up was repeatedly destroyed by gangs, and that broke him. But in another sense they failed, because his widow Anne, undefeated, took up painting, with success. One of her pictures, of Westminster, was bought by a former Government Minister, now a peer. And her son Anthony — 'Mitch' — an expert in videographics and formerly with the BBC, now runs his own 'moving pictures' company in London.

Chapter 20

FAMOUS DYNASTY

Mansion where even the servants had servants

Some famous people and families go to great lengths to guard and preserve their privacy. The great Guinness and Iveagh 'dynasty' did so for years — their leading members were, after all, close friends of the Royal Family. At one stage the Guinesses were even a bit shy about advertising their product, the basis of all their fame! When I put forward the idea for a big series 'The Famous Guinness Family — the Most Fascinating Success Story of the Century' colleagues warned, "Don't be too optimistic — they'll never wear that." But, to my joy, the family gave their co-operation — the first time a newspaperman had succeeded in obtaining this — and as 'openers' I was invited to lunch with the firm's board of directors at St. James's Gate, Dublin.

Most memorable of all were the visits to Elveden Hall, the great family mansion in Suffolk, and the meetings with the then 83-year-old Rupert Guinness, second Earl of Iveagh, and his wife Gwendolen — touring the 23,000 acre estate with them in their old Citroën and exploring the vast mansion. It was mainly through these two remarkable personalities that the wonderful family story became alive.

"We're just simple farmers now," they insisted as they recalled the great days of Elveden, bought by the first Earl. He was reckoned — with a fortune of £200,000,000 at today's values — to be the second wealthiest man in England, at that time.

Under his 'rule' Elveden — where King Edward VII was a frequent visitor — was then virtually a private palace. It was the visible symbol of the astonishing success of one of the most extraordinary families that these islands have produced — a family that began with a tiny brewery in Dublin and created a dynasty of untold wealth.

Elveden was once occupied by the Maharajah Duleep Singh after the British Government deposed him from his throne following the Sikh revolt in the Punjab. One of the most striking features of the place is the Indian Hall, an enormous room, all in white marble with lavish carved pillars and Eastern ornamentation. "My father added this hall on after he bought Elveden," said Lord Iveagh. "King Edward nicknamed it the

Taj Mahal."

Because the King was so regular a visitor, the old Lord Iveagh invented a travelling kitchen which followed Edward and his party when they went out shooting. He invented, too, a huge travelling marquee which was quickly erected wherever the early part of the day's shooting was likely to finish. It was heated and had real windows and a perfect wooden floor.

I recall Lord Iveagh remarking as we looked at the walls hung with magnificent Bayeux and Gobelin tapestries, pictures by Gainsborough and Romney and other masters, "All this belongs to a world that has gone. I'm afraid it's a white elephant now."

Under dust covers were stacks of carpets, Sheraton, Louis XIV and other rare furniture. There was the bedroom with the four-poster used by Edward VII and his dressing-room entered by a concealed door. Underneath the mansion was a great strong-room with priceless plate and pictures. Elveden's treasures, worth a score of fortunes, were protected by an elaborate security system. Wires from all rooms connected with alarm bells in local police stations.

I wondered then: What's going to happen to all this colossal wealth of treasures — and to this fantastic mansion where kings and queens, millionaires, lords and ladies once made merry; where even the servants had servants. The visiting ladies' maids were waited upon by footmen as they dined.

The answer came, in part, years later in 1984, when the third Lord Iveagh put his predecessor's enormous and diverse collection up for auction. The 3,297 lots formed the greatest and richest list of possessions sold from any single great house since the Second World War — the cataclysm that ended the Elveden way of life, along with so much else.

During that war, the mansion was occupied for a time by American troops. "There was usually a queue of men anxious to use King Edward's former bathroom," recalled old Lord Iveagh. "It had gold fittings, but some of these were later found to have disappeared."

At our last meeting, he gave me some books about life at Elveden which I still treasure, and it was due to his hard work that the big estate, once the sporting place of millionaires, was transformed into highly productive farmland.

After that series the World's Press News magazine of the time published the following appreciative article headed

WHEN ORR 'DIGS'
SUNDAY DISPATCH
FINDS READERS!

'Has the art of digging hard for news or features died out as some of the critics of the press say? For the benefit of youngsters, I interviewed Charles Orr, Northern news editor of the *Sunday Dispatch*, in Manchester.

'There may be a lot of romance in the fabulous history of the Guinness family in the past 200 years, but Charles found it took a great deal of hard work to dig out the facts for a first-class series of articles in the *Sunday Dispatch*.

'During five weeks he spent researching he had to read 50 books and interview more than 70 people.

'There is no central source of information about the Guinness family. They shunned publicity for many years.

'Charles had to pay visits to the National Library of Ireland, Trinity College Library, and Marsh's Library, one of the oldest libraries in the world, where Dean Swift spent a lot of time.

'The library contains books which bear his satirical annotations written on the side of pages. Another place he had to visit was the Library of the Royal Dublin Society and the Genealogical Office.

'Old newspapers of the 18th and 19th century were housed in the National Library, and he also had to wade through piles of Dublin Corporation minutes.

'He paid a flying trip to Elveden, Suffolk, the great pile built by Maharajah Duleep Singh in the 19th century.

'Charles went there to interview Lord and Lady Iveagh. Lord Iveagh is the chairman of Guinness's, and a great-great-grandson of the first Arthur, who founded the "Guinnesty" with £100 200 years ago.

'He also saw Lord Moyne, vice-chairman of Guinness's, and had lunch with him and other directors at St James's Gate where the first Arthur started the Guinness brewery. This was the first time any journalist has dined there with Lord Moyne.

'Charles also interviewed Lady Patricia Lennox-Boyd, wife of the present Colonial Minister, and daughter of Lord Iveagh.

'Another trip he made was to Celbridge in County Kildare where the first Arthur discovered the secret of making Guinness — according to the books by accidentally burning barley.

'He found during his researches that someone with his own family name, Orr, figured in the Guinness family. He was a Co Down rector who married a Guinness. If Charles could prove his relationship — well he might be on free Guinness for the rest of his life!'

*　　*　　*

And then — an exclusive interview with a legendary personality, a man whose exploits had stirred me since boyhood — famous man of action, ex-Royal Marine, former spy, celebrated writer, poet, playwright, critic — and witty connoisseur of whisky . . .

"I've been drinking whisky and smoking regularly for more than fifty years — and I'm sound as a bell," said Sir Compton Mackenzie one of the most gifted of men.

The one-time intelligence agent, when I said my favourite whisky was Bushmills exclaimed: "Never mind, you can make whisky almost anywhere, but the two ingredients that make good Scotch whisky are inimitable — Scottish barley and our wonderful Highland streams."

When I mentioned the great variety of whiskies one saw in the Highlands he said the springs and streams each had their own distinctive flavour — and every Scotsman, especially every Highlander, was an expert on the subject.

As for smoking, Sir Compton declared that if tobacco vanished from the earth the world would soon be at war again. (So that's why there's been no Third World War?)

He made me look at his tonsils — "See how stained brown they are? They act as filters, you see." He didn't believe that smoking should be so greatly blamed for lung cancer. In 50 years he'd smoked half a ton of tobacco. It was the big worriers who mostly got cancer — if all the cancer talk were true the human race would have been obliterated.

A marvellous character — who else could come out with a throw-away line like this — "I lost my half-moon dyed monkey skin tobacco pouch during a boar hunt in the forest of Compiegne.' Wow!

His three Siamese cats looked up surprised. They mustn't have heard that before. He introduced me to them — Bluebell, Pippo and Pinky Puff. They were loafing on a couch like any ordinary cats.

But Pinky Puff rose and stretched herself with a pleased look as Sir Compton — then President of the Siamese Cat Club — observed, "Cats are superior to dogs because they are more tolerant of tobacco." Purrs of satisfaction all round.

*　　*　　*

That interview with Sir Compton Mackenzie occurred during one of many visits to Scotland — and what finer place can there be to visit? Or what finer people? The first assignment which took me there, to the Highlands, was a now-it-can-be-revealed feature series dealing mainly with two wartime spies. They had been working in Norway for the Germans who decided to send them to the United Kingdom to act as secret agents.

In reality the two were pro-Allied. Having been given their orders they were put on a Nazi seaplane which one dark night flew across the North Sea and transferred the couple, along with folding bicycles, to a rubber dinghy in the Moray Firth. The seaplane took off and the two 'spies', in pitch blackness and a gathering storm, had no idea where land was. Half-frozen they managed to get ashore at the foot of a cliff at Crovie, near Macduff, in Banffshire. They hammered with their revolver butts on the door of an isolated cottage, but the occupants, an elderly couple, spotting the weapons, slammed the door in their faces — they thought it was the start of a German invasion!

The feature went on to describe how the two 'spies' were captured, taken under guard to London, and had great difficulty in convincing the authorities that they were in fact pro-British. Eventually their story was verified and the two were retrained, equipped and set up as double-agents, sending back false information to their German 'bosses'.

Along with other spy goings-on at that time this story — with many interviews and pictures — made a first-class and exciting feature series. But to my dismay the 'top brass' in Whitehall banned it under the Official Secrets Act — ostensibly on the grounds that the information and details it revealed would be helpful to an enemy in the event of a future war!

An official communication from Whitehall which I saw at the time contained this paragraph:

'Confidential — The work of Superintendent — (mentioned in my story) brought him into touch with double-agents whom we employed. Our Security authorities are absolutely adamant that the activities of these gentlemen must be kept secret. The men to whom you refer as — (names) were very much concerned.'

A great deal of work had been put into that feature and its loss was a bitter disappointment — I've never had the heart to throw away the copy.

Another feature series with a strong Scottish interest (which did get past Whitehall) was the story of 'Wee McGrigor' — Admiral Sir Rhoderick McGrigor, the hero of the Sicily landings and veteran of Jutland and the Dardanelles — a warrior who at sea always slept under his clan tartan rug. One of the stories related in this series concerned a young man always addressed as 'Johnson' who in wartime fought in the gun-turret of a battleship. He was in fact the future King George the Sixth.

This feature covered the drama of the sinking of the *Bismarck* and many other naval exploits. Former admirals, captains and old sea-dogs in Scotland and England gave great help with their recollections of stirring events when the war situation was touch and go. They included Admiral Sir Patrick Brind, former C-in-C Allied Forces Northern Europe; Admiral Sir William Wellclose Davis, former NATO C-in-C Eastern Atlantic; Rear-Admiral Hugh Faulkner, who was McGrigor's Chief of Staff during the Sicily landings; Admiral Sir Geoffrey Alan Brooke Hawkins, who was captain of the warship *Kent* during McGrigor's Norwegian operations; Capt. Kenneth Short, who commanded the aircraft carrier *Campania* on the Russian convoy routes, and Rear-Admiral Godfrey ('Ben') Teale, Chief Staff Officer C-in-C., who served with McGrigor for 17 years. Wonderful personalities all of these, and they were kind enough later to express appreciation of the series.

*   *   *

Everybody loves a lord, so they say — but this may not always be strictly true. Some, like Lord Hailsham, the former journalist (*Daily Mail* man) Lord Killanin, Lord Whitelaw and Lord (Gerry) Fitt can be affable and forthcoming — but others are occasionally unhelpful if not downright stupid or ill-mannered.

Of scores of noblemen interviewed my outstanding personality is the cheerful and wealthy Duke of Westminster — not because of his millions (he is said to be 'worth' £1,400 million) but for his character, humour and general attitude to life. When he was a seven-year-old boy he kept a money-box into which he put a two-shilling piece every Saturday.

We kicked around then on the lawn with a football, and his sisters joined in. Such an interview with such a young heir would never be permitted in today's conditions — for security reasons and fears of kidnapping. The headlines and picture captions then featured 'The soccer-loving lad who will inherit £1,400 millions — and a big chunk of London.'

At that time, twirling a toy-gun, he told me that he intended to be a soldier in the Foreign Legion one day. His elder sister interrupted to remind him that the previous week he had determined to be a taxi-driver, and his younger sister Jane told him his ambition had been to live in a caravan. But young Gerald Grosvenor, as he was known then, picked up a watering hose and shouted into the nozzle: "I've changed my mind. Can you hear me girls? This is my telephone."

He still has that money-box but now, at 37 the fourth richest person in Britain — who inherited also his parents' sense of duty — devotes much of his time and money to helping the NSPCC. "I remember how lucky I was as a child to have such a good home and such good parents," he says. "Today cruelty to the young is rife throughout the country regardless of class."

* *

"Who the hell would want to see me in the nude?"
— actor Richard Burton interviewed after he had
a row with a director over a new film.

* *

In contrast, the most introvert and reluctant nobleman encountered was the man who became the seventeenth Lord Winchester, Richard Charles Paulet. When, being a cousin, he succeeded — as 'Premier Marquess of England'— to the famous title dating back to 1551 he was a bachelor aged 60 and living with his mother in a small semi-detached house.

One would have expected at such a time to find the new marquess in great form, laughing, looking forward to taking his seat in the Lords — "Hello, how are you? What will you have to drink?"— that sort of thing.

But no — not this heavy shambling gentleman whose predecessors had been pals of kings and queens dating back to Henry the Eighth and the first Elizabeth. His demeanour was more like that of an undertaker who'd just heard he'd gone bankrupt. Not a smile, scarcely a word and each of those seemingly a severe effort.

He appeared to be terrified of his mother, an old lady of rather domineering appearance who kept a keen eye on him. After a time when we both glanced at her she took the hint and left the sitting-room. Alone at last — but her authority and influence must still have been weighing upon him as he fidgeted and shuffled during what passed as an interview.

The title? Marquess? Premier Marquess of England? Ah, yes — the title — just so. One succeeds in such cases — true, true. Yes, indeed — very true. The House of Lords — ah, indeed. Interesting place, they say. A seat in the House of Lords? Extraordinary — very strange business. Take my seat in the Lords? Very odd. Perhaps not. A bit inconvenient. Travelling — that sort of thing.

After all this illumination maybe he would have something equally fascinating to reveal on the subject of possible marriage.

Marriage? He started with shock at such an idea. Ah, hum, perhaps, perhaps not. Extraordinary thing. Unlikely — strange business. Don't think so now — ah, no. And a nervous glance towards where SHE was listening.

Later at a local shop the woman behind the counter was chatting to customers about, guess what — "The premier MARSHAL of England" — the new luminary in their midst — "He's scared stiff of his old mum, y'know — at his age. I saw him the other day squinting like a schoolboy round the corner of the garden wall at the end of his road to see if she was coming back — and then he hurried away in case she spotted him."

Ah, hum, yes indeed. Strange business. Takes all sorts, doesn't it?

But there's a new 'premier marquess' now.

Reverting to the Duke of Westminster, although he owns half of Mayfair, all of Belgravia and lands in Cheshire, Shropshire, Wales and Ireland, he is a long way behind Britain's richest person the Queen — and she is a long way ahead of the next richest, Sir John Moores, the one-time Post Office messenger who founded Littlewoods Pools and mail-order firm, and Garry Weston, the foods group boss.

There are an estimated 20,000 millionaires and seven billionaires in the United Kingdom — among them a surprising number of singers and comedians. But not all of the super-rich of the recent past found much to sing about or to laugh about. One of these once told me how he began life as a penniless 'mucker-out' in a mine. Multi-millionaire Chester Beatty, born in New York of Scottish descent, became fascinated with geology early in life and spent hours collecting and studying mineral stones.

"I was not much more than a kid, with nothing to lose, so I started off for the Rocky Mountains," he said. "Like many others I had to begin there the hard way — clearing away muck and debris to earn my bread. But I never doubted that one day I'd strike it rich. I believe that if you want something vitally important to you you'll succeed if you work at it hard enough."

He did strike it rich, of course, although he suffered and risked his life among the peaks and ravines of the Rockies and in Mexico. The day came when others said of him "That guy can smell hidden wealth under the earth." And in the face of scepticism he 'smelt' the potentiality of copper fields in Rhodesia — eventually they were producing vast riches.

When he died at 92 in Monte Carlo Sir Alfred Chester Beatty left art treasures, paintings and rare books worth many millions of pounds.

Most of these titled personages were polite and courteous — except for one lady, a princess in fact — Her Serene Highness Princess Marie-Gabrielle Sophie Joti Elisabeth Albertine Almeria of Wurttemburg! She was at the time wife of the Hon. Desmond Walter Guinness, of Leixlip Castle, Co. Kildare — a gentleman. She was so rude one day on the telephone that *he* wrote to me later apologizing.

'I hope that you will forgive her' his letter concluded. (It's not every day one is asked by the son of a peer to forgive a princess!)

The two were divorced later — not, of course, because of the phone incident but for personal reasons.

Chapter 21

IN COUNTY DOWN . . .

Story of sea disaster that brought back memories

One of the most difficult features to handle was an anniversary series describing in great detail the disaster which befell the cross-Channel vessel *Princess Victoria*. It was a story recording minute by minute the terrible tragedy that overtook the ship in a gale on 31 January, 1953, with the loss of 133 lives. All the women and children perished. The *Princess Victoria* went down while trying to make her regular Stranraer to Larne crossing.

A dramatic story was eventually put together with the co-operation of Stanley Shivas — 'our man in Glasgow' — but we were relieved when it was over. Many of the scores of people approached slammed doors in our faces, some were abusive, and a few complained of 'intrusion into grief'. Photographers, too, were given a hard time.

The one bright spot then was interviewing the lifeboat crew at Donaghadee, Co. Down. Coxswain the late Hugh Nelson and his men saved 34 of the *Princess Victoria's* survivors in their worst day for 43 years.

It was a nostalgic experience for me being back in my old home town and recalling that one of the lifeboatmen, Alex Nelson, later Coxswain, had once fished me out of the harbour when as a youngster I fell off the greasy pole during a summer regatta.

Alex had been a boyhood hero then when, after big storms, bodies of seamen were on occasion washed up on the beaches or into the harbour. He often took me and my pals Willie Kenny, his brother Gerald Kenny, Billy Louden and others over to the Copeland Islands where we went 'rabbiting' and swimming. He sometimes lay on his back on the deck singing in the sunshine while the big motor boat chugged on her course unattended. "Sure she knows the way better than any of us," he laughed.

In later years poems were written in honour of Alex and his prowess.

Willie Kenny — later as Lieutenant William Kenny — was awarded the Victoria Cross posthumously. The Kenny boys' mother and my own mother were long-time friends. Sometimes when they discussed times past we would hear of dramatic incidents such as the 'gun-running'.

In that episode the Unionist Volunteers one night secretly unloaded thousands of rifles and ammunition from a vessel in the harbour. Other consignments were landed at Bangor and Larne. It was estimated that up to 50,000 rifles and 3,000,000 rounds were distributed at the three ports. It was a highly organized operation, said my mother, and all carried out in darkness with speed and efficiency. Sadly, however, she added that my father's death some years later was an indirect result of the ordeal of that night and subsequent strains. He was the officer in charge of police in the area and, with his men, was held captive on the quayside during the incident. My mother bravely went to the harbour, which was ringed by Volunteers, and after a time was permitted to hand over coffee and sandwiches to my dad and others. After the gun-running there was political uproar and the Government sent destroyers to patrol the coast — a little late! Then the Government, affronted at having been caught napping, ordered an inquiry. Army, Navy and police chiefs were interrogated. (Where had the Secret Service been all the time?) My father was one of those whose health broke under the strain of the time and he died in hospital aged only 51.

My mother received no compensation or pension — not even a letter of condolence — from the authorities on the loss of her husband. But she never allowed herself to become embittered, never complained, except at times to toss her head with scorn and remark, "Oh, what do you expect?" on hearing of some instance of insensitive officialdom.

"It was a famous incident of history, of course, but he and you and I suffered," she said. "Your father would be alive today had it not been for what happened. He did not suffer the same fate as William Orr, but the result was the same — he lost his life."*

The loss of her husband was the second great blow my mother had suffered, the first being the death of her little daughter Ethel. But, as mentioned earlier, she started a guest-house and, with no help whatever from any earthly source, she worked unremittingly and made a new life for herself and me. It was only years later that I fully realized and appreciated all that she had overcome and achieved.

---

* She was referring to William Orr, who after an infamous trial was hanged on the Gallows Green at Carrickfergus on 14 October, 1797 on a trumped-up charge of administering the oath of the United Irishmen.

Some of his relatives were among many of the same name who fled to America after that, landed at New Castle, Delaware, and later founded Orrville, now an industrial town in Wayne County 45 miles south of Cleveland, Ohio.

But that's another story — that perilous Atlantic voyage of many weeks in those sailing-ship times, then the 400-mile trek by men, their wives and families through Delaware, Maryland, West Virginia, Pennsylvania, Ohio . . .

She had a great sense of humour and used to poke gentle fun at people who grumbled needlessly. "They don't know when they're well off," she said. "Think of poor Mrs Elliot."

Mrs Elliot, a widow, had a grown-up son and daughter, both crippled. My mother sometimes went round to their house in Killaughey Road to lend a hand. Later I went too. It impressed one to see how they managed. In the hall and along the stairs and in the rooms many hand-grips had been screwed into the walls. Teddy, the son, and his twin sister Nelly, in their late teens, dragged themselves about quite rapidly. As well as being crippled their speech was slightly affected. But both were highly intelligent and well read. They were always in good humour, never grumbled, never showed any embarrassment or even awareness of their plight.

When I remarked on this my mother commented: "They have nobility. They work at being vital and cheerful. They don't want pity. They want to make their mother's task easier. It's a lesson to everyone." She told me that the parents of the two had been first cousins. Some years later the twins died within a short while of each other, and shortly afterwards the mother went too. A hard-hit family — but I remember their home as a bright and happy place.

A bright and happy place, too, is how one remembers Donaghadee — the lovely old seaport whose stones and beaches could tell a colourful story dating from pre-Christian times. Its important role in Ulster's development over the centuries is part of the theme of Sam Hanna Bell's novel *Across the Narrow Sea*.

A wonderful place in which to grow up. And, funny, the things one recalls on returning — the schoolmaster Mr Lamont guiding my infant hand in his own to write my name, a magic moment as the Vere Foster-style letters appeared miraculously from MY fingers; Billy Louden and I at eight years old spluttering over our first Woodbines on top of the Moat; getting trapped by incoming tide in a cavern and just escaping waist-deep to safety; joining the townsfolk searching for a lost child — later found drowned in the pond behind the old Baths Hotel; the circus band parading through the town — clowns, lions, elephants and all — then with my pals tunnelling under the canvas walls of the 'big top' to watch the show.

The sea, the beaches, islands, boats, rocks and caves were an unending fascination. The storms, too. Huge 'walls' of waves soared across the Parade, where we lived and spray streamed down the window panes. The beaches were strewn with cargo of all kinds when big ships foundered. Once we helped recover a missing seaman's body from the harbour. One of his legs was missing and for days afterwards Billy and I vied with theories about this.

At Christmas time we trailed around in the wake of the 'mummers', bands of traditional revellers or entertainers who went from house to house. Some adorned themselves with horns or false heads to resemble animals or birds. Others wore fantastic costumes and grinning masks. They made 'music' with tin whistles, tambourines, Jew's harps and mouth-organs. I can still see them and hear them — to us they were strange, exciting, unpredictable and wonderful.

Once we followed them into the day-room of the local police station. I remember their rhyming and capers being punctuated by shouting and banging from the cells where disorderly drunks were kicking the heavy doors in the fuddled hope of being set free.

The visit recalled a verse from a poem by Rosamond Lloyd Praeger:

In County Down — where I live — the sea sweeps by.
Far above the ploughlands the white gulls fly.
Bees in the clover, honey in the air —
Oh, County Down is beautiful, and I live there.

*   *   *

All this old-home-town nostalgia was soon eclipsed by work on other features — Josef Locke and his problems, not to mention a series of you wouldn't-believe-it adventures. Like getting locked accidentally inside a round tower, a story about monks and young women living together on a trawler, interviewing a 14-year-old bride, wife of a travelling man, whose home was a caravan, and helping to rescue a horse which had fallen through the floor of an old castle. This castle, in Co. Galway, was being restored and renovated by a young woman relative of Viscount Gort, and from what she told me the horse incident was one of the least of the problems involved in the restoration work.

Amusing enough adventures in their way — but one story that followed soon afterwards resulted in so much 'hassle' that I wished I'd never bothered. It led to my becoming involved in a time-consuming, seemingly endless inquiry involving — dandelions and women's busts!

It all began innocently with a brief story about tablets made from dandelion roots in Japan which, it was claimed, had the effect of increasing the size of the bust. Should amuse some readers, I thought.

Then — oh, dear — an avalanche of letters from women all over England, Ireland, Scotland, Wales. Even some from Belgium, Germany and Italy. (Italy? I had thought Italian women were all OK in that area.)

Some of the anxious ladies went into detail about their statistics. Some even enclosed photographs. The editor wasn't impressed when I said maybe a 'bust secretary' should be appointed. "You looking for a bosom friend?" he laughed. "Why not open a clinic?"

My problem was: how to track down those tablets. Endless inquiries — with research laboratories, wholesale chemists, industrial chemists, consulting chemists, manufacturing chemists, trade connections, university laboratories, herbal shops, botanical experts, vegetable experts. Then — Telex messages to Tokyo, inquiries with export boards, even the trade section boss of the Japanese Embassy.

Comical comments, of course, from one and all but no luck. I told myself: "You're a right eejit for running that story."

So . . . off with replies to all the ladies — 'Regret unable to trace these particular tablets at the moment — inquiries continuing — however, during investigations have found out about other products recommended for the same purpose: an instant dandelion coffee compound, protein tablets, and herbal drinks.'

Lost a bit of weight myself over that episode. I suppose the moral is: little things can mean a lot — of work. (Or, as my friend Gay Byrne, the TV presenter once observed: "Nothing anyone may say or do can suprise me now.")

*   *   *

Often the stories that DON'T get into the paper provide a laugh — like the circus woman acrobat and her saucy antics with the ringmaster — how she put him through the hoop! And the bogus bishop in his flowing robes who could talk people into parting with their cash. A photographer colleague and I took him up to the 'palace' of a real bishop — where there was a somewhat unepiscopal scene after he tried to sweet-talk the housekeeper. Then the troubles that befell a lonely spinster who invented a 'sexy wig' and combined love-potion-hair-restorer for old baldies.

And the tragic-comic story of a deserted wife and her runaway husband who after a brandy session staged a repeat church ceremony of their own. He asked her for the wedding ring which he knew she still carried about in her handbag. He placed the ring on her finger again as he had done twenty years previously, told her that he loved her best of all. But afterwards over more drinks in an hotel he suddenly rushed off — to be with the 'other' woman. And the again-deserted wife said "I still love him — I wish I didn't."

A spell of working, along with Peter Earle, on the Kim Philby spy story — and then one day a voice out of the past suddenly came over the phone. It was that of Baillie Stewart, better known as the 'Officer in the Tower'. He was a Guards captain who had years earlier been imprisoned in the Tower of London for treason after having been on 'leave' in Berlin. He was later dismissed from the Army in disgrace.

He was now calling from a pub, said he had a 'great story' and we must meet to discuss it. We made an appointment for that evening — at the same pub. When we met he looked as if he had never left the place. The one-time Guards officer had now became a pitiable sight — shabby, down at heel and ingratiating. And the story he was offering? It was about William Joyce — 'Lord Haw-Haw' — who broadcast from Berlin to Britain during the war and whose apparently detailed knowledge of events on occasion caused speculation. He explained that he had known Joyce very well and that he had 'a lot to tell'. First, he wanted money — a considerable sum. We talked for the rest of the evening and it became clear there was no new and sensational story forthcoming. He seemed a lonely figure at that stage, still dominated by the dramatic episode in which he had once been the central character. But unhappily for him no newspaper had now any time for him or wished to re-hash the affair. He died a few years later.

This was an uneasy but eventful period — between the murder of the British Ambassador Christopher Ewart-Biggs in 1976 and of Airey Neave almost three years later — a huge variety of stories: interviewing Russian Ambassador Kaplin about alleged 'Red' spying activities; claims by Transcendental Meditiation 'gurus' about being able to fly unaided; the prison wedding of Eddie Gallagher and heiress Dr Rose Dugdale; 'Jackie' Kennedy, and, of course, the activities of 'the Boss' Charles Haughey, a politician seldom out of the headlines.

But one of the most interesting stories was that told me by 'Beatles widow' Cynthia . . .

Chapter 22

CYNTHIA'S 'SHOCK'

Found Yoko and John in their dressing-gowns

Cynthia, the ex-wife of millionaire Beatle John Lennon, told me one day — in June 1978 — how Yoko, the way-out Japanese artist, had 'stolen' her husband. She had not realized until too late that the two had been meeting and corresponding — and then one day on returning to her home in Surrey she found them together in their dressing-gowns, in the morning room, and they merely greeted her, almost contemptuously, with "Oh, hi."

She said she had never previously suspected John of two-timing her — even during the hectic years when the Beatles were on their world tours and surrounded continually by groupies and glamour girls. She first began to feel misgivings after their much publicized visit to the guru Maharishi in India. John then began talking a lot about the 'seven-year itch' and about 'experimenting'. He started taunting her about being naïve.

Cynthia described the circumstances of the break-up with John while she was in my home where I had arranged an 'open' telephone line for most of the day to the *News of the World* office in Fleet Street. We had to be in constant touch with Fleet Street because on that day three leading judges were deciding on John Lennon's attempt to stop Cynthia telling her story to the paper's readers — a serialized version of her book *A Twist of Lennon* published later that month. The judges eventually rejected Lennon's case, including his argument that publication would affect their son Julian.

In between phone calls Cynthia, who was accompanied by her then new husband John Twist, spoke of Yoko without the slightest bitterness — perhaps she regarded the couple as beneath that — and in fact she commented: "I had an instinct at one stage that she was the right person for John — they had the same outlook!" That remark said a lot, I felt.

But after confronting Yoko and John together that morning in their dressing-gowns, she recalled, she was 'in a state of shock', ran upstairs and packed her things. "I had to get away from that scene," she said. But after a time she returned. Yoko had left. She and John had a long talk and it seemed as if there might be a reconciliation. Later, however, he refused to take her with him on a projected trip to America. Cynthia then went with her mother and Julian on an Italian holiday. While she was away Yoko moved in with John and it was while she was still in Italy that she received the news that John had decided on a divorce.

The subsequent murder of her ex-husband in a New York street and later problems appear to have left the level-headed Cynthia undefeated. How did such an attractive, intelligent and art-loving girl come to marry John Lennon in the first place? She smiled and recalled: "He wasn't like that at the start. Things changed completely when the group became so famous and it was a crazy extravagant time for all of us. We were happy and in love once and now I bear no ill-will and no malice."

R. M. Smyllie coping as Editor during the 'Emergency' — a cartoon by Warner.

Chapter 23

DALEY PROPHECY

'ULSTER will suffer the same riot tactics'

Newspapermen's wives have a lot to put up with (in addition to their husbands) and this can include many changes of residence from time to time. Happily my own wife Dorothy put up with all our 'flittings' cheerfully enough — thanks in part to the fact that she herself has a newspaper background. Her father the late W.A.E. (Albert) Withers was for many years Irish correspondent for *The Times* of London and the *Financial Times*, and her brother Kenneth is a former Editor of the *Belfast News-Letter*, Ireland's oldest daily paper. And she has written many articles on musical topics for newspapers and magazines. Our homes over the years included Finchley (Hendon Lane), Speen (Buckinghamshire), Wimbledon (Compton Road), Bayswater (Queen's Gardens), Manchester (Birchfields and Withington), Hale, (Cheshire), Dublin (Montpelier Hill), and Bangor, (Co. Down), — to name a few!

With two small daughters at first to cater for, and, later, two sons — as well as me of course — she found Manchester and Cheshire among the best places for shopping, from a housewife's point of view. She has vivid memories of some of those places where we lived. The house in Wimbledon still had a huge corrugated iron Anderson shelter in the drawing-room — erected and abandoned by the previous owner.

In Buckinghamshire our nearest neighbour was a market gardener and it intrigued us to watch his wife digging and slaving away while he looked on with interest, smoking and giving instructions. In Finchley we had a lovely house, but life was complicated by our housekeeper Bessie, an elderly eccentric, who had a succession of romantic problems, real and imaginary. When all was going swimmingly she was full of beans, bustling about the house and singing. But when there was a rift with her latest lover she became a fury, banging doors, throwing saucepans around the kitchen and snorting with anger. "Bessie's been betrayed again," we groaned.

At another of our homes the local council moved a family of tinkers into a neighbouring house which had fallen vacant. The newcomers included a horde of unruly children, and what with them and groups of their 'visitors' who took up residence for periods, our area which had been a pleasant and quiet residential neighbourhood, became noisy and lawless and the scene of drunken confrontations on occasion. At such times Dorothy might sit down at the piano to charm away disagreeable sounds. Eventually a number of families, including ourselves, sold up and left the district, no other relief being forthcoming. We learned later that the fine old houses had been demolished.

With such experiences my wife had no difficulty in accepting one's frequent departures at short notice to cover stories in various parts of the world. And, to go back a little, so it was — in the mid-sixties when I went to interview Mayor Richard Daley, the legendary and controversial 'Boss' of Chicago. He was at the time one of the most heavily guarded men in the United States — in his big municipal offices and also in his home. He received me at both these places and kindly arranged for an officer and a police car to be put at my disposal during my stay in the city.

During my interviews with him — just after the mob riots at the period of the Democratic National Convention in August 1968 — he explained the lengths to which the demonstrators, or 'Yippies' as they were generally called, had gone to try to smash the convention and, as they had aimed, to create chaos and paralyse the city.

Daley, tough and forthright, was prophetic. The revolutionary new style tactics and weapons used, he said, were a blueprint for international malcontents. "You'll find they will be used in Ulster too."

This American trip was in fact cut short by the 'troubles' in Northern Ireland. Covering the persistent rioting in Derry, Belfast and elsewhere was the start of the longest-running story of all. Week after week the marches and confrontations, and stoning, shooting and fire bombing. Trying to phone copy from call-boxes and being dragged out with kicks, punches and insults, being 'rocked' in one's car by a mob intent on destruction, getting batoned when caught up in sudden charges by police against rioters.

Lucky escapes, too, from two disastrous hotel fires in Derry and one in Belfast. In another hotel, the Charlemont Arms in Armagh — happily still standing — there was a farcical episode when a mob, angered at the banning of a march, suddenly besieged dozens of reporters and photographers who had crowded into the lounges.

"Come on out, you bastards, and fight," they screamed as they threatened to break the door down. But we sensibly declined this invitation and, instead, made for the bar — only to find that it had been closed! Gloom, despair. The pub with no beer available!

The man from the *Daily Telegraph* Charles Henn cried out: "Ah, fill the cup — what boots it to repeat how time is slipping underneath our feet." And the *Sunday Express* chap roared: "Those in the tavern shout: Open then the door. Once departed we may return no more." But the bar remained shut. After a time the mob was dispersed, the bar reopened and another crisis was over.

Television, I believe, must bear some responsibility for the extent of the rioting. Marches and demonstrations became almost a vicious 'sport' in Ulster at that time, especially on Saturdays. Time and again one saw television crews conferring with the march leaders about the hour of the start, the route to be followed, the place of confrontation with the police. Screaming invective, taunting, jeering and spitting at the police, as I had seen in Chicago, were all part of the game. It all made 'good instant television'. The worse the violence the more likely it would be screened in Britain and abroad. A tame peaceful march would not be 'good television'.

At a critical stage of the Ulster 'troubles' I got an interview with Martin McGuinness, then 'Officer Commanding Derry Brigade Provisional IRA' — making me the first newspaperman into the 'No go' enclave of the Bogside. Steel girders had been driven deep into concrete. No British troops or RUC patrols could enter the area, where Republican flags were flying. London newspapers were protesting: 'Part of the United Kingdom has been taken over.'

A friend of McGuinness with whom I had been in contact enabled me to obtain a 'passport' to enter 'Free Derry'. It stated:

> *'This is to certify that Charles Orr has been cleared by the committee and, as a member of the Press, should be treated with every courtesy and given every consideration.'*

The 'passport' was authorized and signed by Mr Paddy Doherty, of the 'Derry Citizens' Defence Association'. This was before the tragedy of 'Bloody Sunday' (30 January, 1972) when 13 civilians were shot by British Paratroopers — and before McGuinness, with others, was flown to London in an RAF aircraft for 'truce talks'. But at that stage the talks had not been arranged.

The meeting place with McGuinness — he was 21 then — turned out to be at the home of his mother. Fair-haired and six feet tall, he talked quietly and dispassionately. How did he decide — as OC — on targets? "I have meetings with company staffs," he said, "and we decide what jobs should be done. We decide how it should be done. The targets are economic and military. Top priority is the safety of the civilian population."

Later in the interview he said: "When the Provos started in Derry there were only five of six volunteers. Now there are hundreds — with thousands of sympathizers, who are as good as volunteers."

I was also the first newspaperman then to witness the rough justice meted out at one of the secret courts operating in the Bogside. The 'chairman of the court' sat in a big armchair in the front room of a terrace house. The 'defendants', two youths, sat on a sofa facing him. They had been caught by a Peace Corps patrol, Bogside's unofficial police, stealing copper piping, it was alleged.

The hearing dragged on in a rambling manner for three hours. During an interval soup and then tea were served to everyone, including the prisoners. Finally the defendants got round to admitting the offences and the chairman announced the court's decision. Officials of the Citizens' Defence Committee were appointed to call on the parents who had to guarantee that the youths would be kept indoors at night and otherwise restricted in their movements.

In cases of theft culprits were ordered to repay the amounts involved. Said Paddy Doherty, "We find that exposure of offences to relatives and imposition of the curfew are effective in most cases."

These 'kangaroo courts' were only one strange aspect of Derry's Bogside 'republic' then. The Peace Corps had their own 'ops room' controlling the Corps' transport, security, finances, medical and housing departments. On the walls of the room were maps and charts, schedules and orders. Officials were always watching for any infringement of their 'territorial rights'. While I was in the room a Corps member rushed in and reported, "RUC patrols are going down Bishop Street to Carrigans Lane." That was in the committee's territory!

Doherty grabbed a phone — a direct line to Lieut-Colonel Charles Millman, Officer Commanding the 1st Battalion Queen's Regiment, who controlled security in the city at that time. He shouted, "Colonel, the police are in our area. If they go down that lane there could be trouble — their safety could be imperilled." After a few more words Doherty put down the phone with a grin. "They won't go that way again," he said. "They must be mad."

While this amazing situation continued people there were still claiming all their social benefits — and Loyalists were demanding, "When is the Army going to move in?"

The No-Go regime in the Bogside was eventually smashed by Operation Motorman — an 'invasion' by British troops in July 1972. It seemed an unbelievable spectacle in what, after all, is part of the United Kingdom — on the ground massive military force, and overhead RAF jets swooping above IRA strongholds. A strange experience being a 'war correspondent' in the Queen's 'back-yard'.

There was an element of comedy surrounding even that dramatic event. I got a tip-off that the then British Ambassador in Ireland — Sir John Peck — whose Embassy in Dublin had been burned down after 'Bloody Sunday' — was dashing around in Co. Cork trying to find Jack Lynch, the Republic's then Prime Minister, to inform him about Operation Motorman! This was at Downing Street's behest.

But Jack Lynch was nowhere to be found. He was taking part in a by-election campaign and his exact whereabouts were difficult to pin down. Phone calls yielded nothing and by now the Ambassador must have been in a diplomatic sweat.

By chance Eire's Foreign Minister Dr Patrick Hillery, (later the President) came to Peck's rescue and was able to contact Lynch and arrange a meeting between the two men. This took place in Cork after midnight and the Ambassador at last was able to inform the Prime Minister of the 'invasion' — Derry's D-Day — starting only a few hours later.

*　　*　　*

'Troops living like pigs' was the title of a feature I wrote at one stage during the Ulster rioting. A Christmas comforts fund was set up and TVs were provided for the men — many of whom had to live in old disused factories.

Despite their non-social life, the men, such as those in the Green Howards, never seemed to lose their sense of humour, and many of their wisecracks have remained:

"We like to spend money on girls, some on beer, some on football boots — and the rest foolishly."

"Sergeant Birdsall looks better without his teeth."

"Bull Winkle Williams can sleep through a bomb attack — no trouble."

"Lance-Corporal Lucas thinks he can have sex with a telephone."

"The food here's great — ask anyone in Musgrave Hospital."
"Corporal Marsden's feet have shrunk."
Some of them invented songs — here's a verse from one:

'I've sweated in the jungle
And suffered the desert's heat
There's nowt I swear that can compare
With the silence of a Belfast street.'

One of the grim features of the period was the manner in which the bombers and gunmen ignored the passionate appeal for peace made by Pope John Paul during his three days in Ireland in 1979. He was the first Pope in history to visit the country where — said the bishops in a pastoral letter — he is "greatly loved". It was a memorable occasion when, amid a sea of waving flags and handkerchiefs, his helicopter landed that afternoon, September 29, at Killineer, Co. Louth, not far from the Border, and he made his dramatic plea — "on my bended knees I beg you" — for an end to the killings. The vast crowd cheered. The Pope was accorded further great welcomes at Dublin, Knock, Galway and Limerick — but his challenge to the gunmen to put an end to their "murdering hates" went unheeded.

A turbulent time then, the seventies, but with a great variety of other news stories, including George Best's supposed romance with Sinead Cusack, Marianne Faithful's supposed romance with Lord Rossmore, taking flowers to Bernadette Devlin (on behalf of the Editor) after she'd had her baby, interviewing Ian Paisley, Maureen O'Hara, Billy Graham.

But the oddest story was 'the women's lib train'.

*   *   *

The 'women's lib train' became famous overnight when a large group of women travelled from Dublin to Belfast on the strangest of shopping sprees — they invaded chemists' shops there and loaded up with supplies of contraceptives and the Pill. Then, carrying banners, they got on to the next train back to Dublin. It was a big protest against Eire's law at that time banning the importation or sale of the Pill or any other contraceptive.

When the women reached Dublin and poured from the train they were greeted by hundreds of Women's Liberation Movement supporters — and a line of police and customs officers. As the women surged forward cheering and shouting there were scuffles with the police. Packets of contraceptives went flying over the barriers and were grabbed by their supporters on the other side.

The officials were confronted by placards reading 'Arrest me — I'm on the Pill' and 'Women are only baby machines'. Some of the women told the customs men, "We've got the Pill," and a few swallowed the tablets when ordered to hand them over.

Others who had their packets of contraceptives confiscated gave their names and addresses and demanded receipts. One woman who refused to surrender her packets eventually succeeded in getting past the officials and was immediately followed by a rush of other 'libbers' who had quickly lined up behind her. The entire party with their cheering supporters then marched out of the station brandishing and waving their packets of contraceptives in triumph.

These goings-on, observed by my colleague Michael Devine were succeeded by what became known as 'the McGee case' — a mother of four eventually obtained a Supreme Court verdict in her favour: that the law, on which customs men had acted, prohibiting the importation of a contraceptive was inconsistent with the constitution.

That court decision forced the state to make it possible for married persons to buy contraceptives in the Republic, if they so wished, on prescription — but today many chemists in the Republic still don't stock contraceptives and some doctors won't write a prescription for them.

Derry Citizens' Defence Association

27 RATHLIN GARDENS, CREGGAN
DERRY.

II SEPT. 1969.

This is to certify that Charle s Orr has been cleared by the committee and as a member of the press should be treated with every courtsy and

given every consideration.

.....*Paddy Doherty*.........

My 'passport' for entry to the Bogside, Londonderry, when the area set up its own 'republic'. Eventually British troops invaded the place and ended the no-go situation.

Chapter 24

FIGHTING TALK

Archbishop's quarrel with 'aggressive' Pope

It's not often one hears 'fighting talk' from a cleric, especially one holding very high office, but I'll never forget the day that an Archbishop no less told me how he had been on the verge of coming to blows with Pope Paul the Sixth! Sounds incredible, but the story was told in the presence of witnesses by the so-called rebel Archbishop Marcel Lefebvre, who allowed me to visit his St Pius X Fraternity seminary which is beautifully situated near Econe in the Swiss Alps.

Lefebvre has frequently been accused of conducting a 'holy war' against the Vatican because of his continued refusal to perform the new Mass. Even now he is still not quite forgiven by the Vatican and the present Pope refused to meet him when he visited Switzerland recently, but he did receive him later at the Vatican.

Tall and dignified Archbishop Lefebvre became quite animated as, sitting in his study, he described the angry scene when the former Pope called him to Rome to account for his disobedience. He said, "Pope Paul astonished me from the very outset of our meeting by the way he became extremely aggressive. He raised his voice angrily and gesticulated constantly. He accused me of subjecting him to attack and he called me a Protestant.

"I replied 'We are only defending the Faith. We can follow you only as the true successor of Peter.' At this His Holiness jumped up and shouted at me. He was waving his arms. He demanded 'What are you trying to do to me? Do you yourself want to take over from me as Pope?'

"I was very shocked by his outburst and by his behaviour, and for a moment I had the unbelievable thought that we were going to come to blows. I asked him not to speak to me like that. I was astounded by his aggressive manner."

Lefebvre said that after a moment he suggested to Pope Paul that he should give the old Mass a chance and asked him to agree to a 'period of experiment with the old ways.' The Pope, he said, eventually cooled down and after a time expressed himself as willing to think over the Archbishop's suggestion.

Lefebvre shrugged as he added, "But nothing ever came of it. The Pope was obviously influenced against this course by his Vatican advisers." Despite their row I noticed that the Archbishop still respected Pope Paul and kept a photograph of him hanging on his study wall.

He introduced me to many of the hundreds of students at Econe, some of them from Britain and Ireland. But they are mainly from France, Germany and America. They explained that they underwent strict orthodox training — no smoking, drinking, radio, television or tape recorders. All had their hair cut short.

"A priest should be something special," Lefebvre emphasized afterwards. "In the old days there was a certain heroism about a priest. Today he has become a 'social administrator' or syndicalist. He has become like any other man. Modern novelties and errors are causing divisions in the Faith."

Lefebvre, who at one stage seemed to be facing excommunication,* later handed over the day-to-day running of the seminary to a younger man.

*　　*　　*

It was a very different story when, a few months later, I visited another so-called seminary, this time in Spain. The investigation ended with myself and my free-lance photographer colleague Charles Fennell being chased through back alleys of Seville by a group of enraged members of a weird religious cult. This sect, which included devotees from many nations, claimed to receive 'personal messages' from Heaven directing their operations. They planned to build huge underground shelters and lay in great stores of food because the world, they had been warned, was about to be destroyed.

They set up a 'mother house' in Seville under a 'superior general', a mysterious figure named Fernando, a reputed seer and visionary, who claimed that Christ had appeared to him and told him that he would be Pope one day. He also claimed to have been stigmatized. I saw many of his followers kissing photographs of Fernando. Some dropped to their knees at mention of his name. Others swayed in a kind of ecstasy. All wore scapulars, monastic vestments of an order set up by Fernando.

The sect appointed scores of 'bishops' and other ranks. Many of these

---

* Archbishop Lefebvre was in fact later excommunicated by Pope John Paul II (in June 1988) after consecrating four bishops in a ceremony at Econe. The Vatican denounced his action as "schismatic".

to whom I spoke had never received any theological training and some scarcely any education. There were 'priests' aged from 16 upwards, alleged abbots, nuns, sisters, altar boys. One 17-year-old youth in full-length robes claimed the title of 'archbishop'. They all assured me that Fernando regularly bled from the 'divine' marks on his hands.

A former civil servant from London, Sister Joyce Martin, said that she had given up a well-paid job to join the sect. "The world will be hit by a ball of fire," she informed me with a smile. "It will happen very soon. The wicked will be destroyed. We will survive. We know." Sister Frances McPatrick Massey, daughter of a Dublin business man, said, "There will be a devastating holy war. We are preparing catacombs and storing food supplies in many nations."

* *

"Many people don't really live — they exist without ever appreciating the great miracle of life. Jonathan Swift understood this when he said: May you live all the days of your life!"
— Sir Compton Mackenzie during an interview.

* *

In the warm orange tree-scented streets of Seville it all seemed fantastic. But devotees from England, America, Australia earnestly assured me that the end was nigh. "Visions have shown people dropping into hell's fires," declared Mrs Mary Duffy, a widow, of Bournemouth. "It's like Sodom and Gomorrah nowadays, isn't it? I mean, all those women and girls who appear in Church in bikinis and such. It will happen very soon, we know. The Costa del Sol and all those horrible evil places will go up."

Then I began asking questions of the 'superior' of the sect's monastery — one Father Fulgentius, a bearded American. Why had the Vatican and the Archbishop of Seville banned the organization? What about the people who claimed to have lost everything because of Fernando and his visions? What about a woman who gave up her possessions amounting to £10,000 and a man who sold everything and lost his job because of him? And could we please have a look at Fernando's bleeding hands?

Reaction was swift. "You are wolves in sheep's clothing," roared

Fulgentius. "No interviews, no photographs. Now leave!" Prelates in their bishops' hats and a horde of young priests milled about us in the narrow alley where the mother house was situated. Some were smoking cigars.

"I wish to talk to Fernando," I insisted. But Fulgentius, crimson with anger, shouted, "Go, go. I order you. No more interviews." And to the priests he commanded, "Don't talk to these journalists — disperse."

With that he stalked into the mother house and slammed the door. I then knocked repeatedly at the door and called through a letter-box that I wished to discuss with Fernando some tape recordings said to have been made during the supposed 'messages from heaven'. I wanted to confront him with a charge that they could have been faked.

Then a crowd of young priests emerged from further down the alley and started racing towards us. We didn't stop to argue. We took to our heels and, running through a honeycomb of alleys, got safely to our hotel.

It was the end of our attempt to get into Fernando's hideaway. But from recent reports he and his followers are still active.

*　　*　　*

After Fernando's goings on it was a relief to have a much more pleasant encounter — with the Queen of the White Witches.

Queen Maeve, looking extremely attractive indeed despite the alarming dagger she wielded as part of her regal accoutrements, was in war-like mood at that stage. She had just been elected Queen at a meeting of fellow witches — sorry, sister witches — and she was vowing to wipe out the 'wicked black covens'.

It seems there are more of these covens and witches kicking about than most of us imagine. Some of your best friends could be witches — so watch it!

Anyway, Queen Maeve — she's really Janet Farrar, who runs a coven with her husband Stewart — was resolved that the black witches of this earth must be smoked out and destroyed. Why? Because they're corrupting and vicious, she says, and because they get their kicks through drugs, sex orgies and the sacrificial slaying of animals. They were 'a menace' because many people are fascinated by the occult.

And the white witches? "We use our skills for healing." Covens include housewives, business men, farmers, salesmen — all sorts. They are not recruited but join voluntarily through introductions.

What about those weird rituals — naked dancing and strange

ceremonials one hears about? Mr Farrar explained that they practised a beautiful naked dance rite called Skyclad — "Seems natural to us — nothing salacious — but newcomers can wear a robe at first if they wish."

And then there is THE GREAT RITE — a mysterious sexual ritual. This takes place between a couple — usually husband and wife, or 'established lovers' — who intend to found a new coven, or between a High Priest and Priestess.

The Great Rite can be actual or purely symbolic. It's left to the couple concerned to choose. Afterwards nobody asks the couple whether consummation took place during the ritual.

*   *   *

The type of story newpapermen dislike most is a kidnap — it involves so much waiting and watching with no opportunity to relax.

After the summer of 1974 — beginning with Lord and Lady Donoughmore — armed gangs increasingly resorted to this type of crime. The seizure of Dr Tiede Herrema, the Dutch industrialist, captured the world headlines in 1975.

That kidnap lasted for five weeks and culminated in the long siege of a house in Monasterevin, 40 miles from Dublin. From many parts of the world pressmen and television crews set up 'camp' as police ringed the house. At night arc-lights illuminated the scene and there were flurries of activity from time to time when it was thought Herrema or one of his kidnappers, Eddie Gallagher or Marion Coyle, might be at the upstairs windows.

The concentration of newspapermen and television people became so great that hotels were booked out for miles around. Mobile 'homes' were used by many teams. Temporary lines hooked them into the telephone system. As it was a 'constant watch' job we started camp fires to dispel the midnight chill. Old colleagues around the flames included Alan Whittaker, Steve Valentine, Nicholas Light, Barry Powell, David Roxan and television's globe-trotting Desmond Hamill.

The ordeal of Herrema was severe, but when interviewed after Gallagher and Coyle surrendered, he made light of it — his morale was greater than that of his captors.

It was the kidnap menace and concern for the safety of his wife Carole and their family that induced the famous author Frederick Forsyth to sell his manor house with its 28 acres in Co. Wicklow and move to the south of England. He had bought the place a few years before kidnapping became so frequent, for more than £100,000.

But Carole, a Northern Ireland girl who became a West End actress, happy at first in the country, grew nervous after the Donoughmore and Herrema affairs. And with reason. After all, she is the wife of the man who made millions out of his brilliant thrillers *Day of the Jackal, The Odessa File* and *The Dogs of War*.

During her husband's absences on business from their home Kilgarron House she would never open the front door to strangers but went upstairs. There at the touch of a switch all doors could be locked automatically and she would then open a window and look down at whoever had rung the door bell. If she did not know the callers personally they were asked to leave the property immediately.

One could never forget the fateful year 1979 which involved so many big stories. It began literally with a bang — fifty deaths when the tanker *Betelgeuse* blew up at Whiddy Island.

Then followed the car bomb murder of Mr Airey Neave — Margaret Thatcher became Britain's first woman Prime Minister — Ian Paisley caused uproar at Strasbourg by shouting down Eire's Jack Lynch — then the murder of Lord Louis Mountbatten, the Queen's uncle — a supposed Provo threat to Jim Callaghan — the deaths of 18 soldiers in a bomb trap — the Pope's pilgrimage to Ireland to appeal for an end to the killings — a scare about the IRA photographing Buckingham Palace.

In between this lot there was, a host of light-relief stories — the priest who promised me he would find husbands for lonely girls (what was wrong with them? — Anyway, he never did) — the lover who cast an 'evil spell' — a row over nude scenes in a church group's play — the young widow pestered by her 'demon barber' lover who often hid in the bushes outside her bungalow — the meetings of street girls trying to form their own 'trade union' — and myself getting involved in a row at an embassy after the disappearance of a Dutch girl while on holiday.

The murder of Mountbatten on that lovely day in August — his boat *Shadow V* was blown up by remote control — was not the first attempt on his life. Just fifteen months previously, I discovered, an IRA gunman had lain in wait at the same spot at Mullaghmore, Co. Sligo, as the earl moved about his boat. With his finger on the trigger the sniper watched through a telescopic sight. But because of gusty winds and the choppy water he was unable to line up his target accurately.

Lord Louis must have known that he was on the Provos' death list — but he repeatedly brushed aside security precautions, even after the murder of his friend Airey Neave. On the very morning before he boarded the boat he disregarded an appeal from another friend Mr Hugh Tunney — who sensed danger — that he should put off the trip.

Mr Tunney — who at one stage leased the 27-roomed Classybawn Castle where Mountbatten and members of his family spent many holidays — told me, "I had dinner with Lord Mountbatten at the castle on the Sunday evening. I was not thinking of any bomb attacks when I mentioned my fears to him. I was thinking of all those who had perished in the Fastnet yacht race earlier and I had reservations about his trip. I expressed the fear to him that his boat could sink if conditions became really bad.

"But Lord Mountbatten brushed the warning aside and replied that the boat was one of the safest he could think of. Before going on board he insisted that photographs should be taken of all the group. As the boat left I waved goodbye to him from the pier. If he had any premonition of the disaster that was to follow he gave no hint of it to me. He had absolutely no fear of death."

Mr Tunney attended the funeral at Westminster Abbey.

* * *

Not all interviews were so agreeable as some of the foregoing. For example, a sensational but unpleasant encounter with a young man responsible for starting a furore over the activities of a Tory MP, who was at the centre of homosexual allegations and eventually resigned his parliamentary seat.

This interview, at which I was accompanied by the late Bill St Leger, the well-known press photographer, took place at the Gresham Hotel, Dublin. The young man went there after being asked to leave the MP's London flat where neighbours had told of late-night rows and the sound of smashing glass and crockery.

He claimed during the interview that he had been living with the MP for several years.

"We had rows over other men," he said. "The MP footed all the bills anywhere we went. We travelled around a lot, not politically but socially. I've been on trips to New York, India and France. I was in Greece for a month. He paid all expenses. He was my banker."

After they had had a row, he said, the MP had given him a £700 pay-off.

The MP Mr Harvey Procter described the statements as 'pure character assassination' — but later, after meetings of his constituents, he resigned his parliamentary seat.

Chapter 25

BOURKE'S SECRETS

'Others' who assisted in spy Blake's escape

There are some personalities who carry around with them an aura of mystery that envelops them like a cloak. Sean Bourke, the man behind the springing of the master spy George Blake, was one of these. And, more than six years after his sudden death on a lonely track in County Clare, I am still not entirely convinced that he died from natural causes as then claimed. His body was found in January 1982.

Bourke was a man of secrets and I know that he feared death. He carried his secrets around with him in a brief-case from which he never parted. He also carried a revolver which he showed me saying, "I need this for my protection."

In the brief-case were manuscripts and personal papers, he said, which contained 'sensational disclosures' connected with Blake's escape which he had deliberately left out of his earlier book *The Springing of George Blake*. He said these documents named men and women members of an organization in Britain involved in the escape and described how these people helped raise money to shelter Blake in London, then smuggle him out of England hidden in a van.

Soon after Bourke's sudden death some distance from the caravan which he occupied near Kilkee the brief-case and other belongings of his vanished and have never been traced.

Bourke a short while previously had contacted me with a scheme to give himself up to the British authorities and sell his serialized story to the *News of the World* for £30,000. He had been living aimlessly in Dublin and Limerick for some years after the Irish courts refused to extradite him to Britain. Most of his time and money he spent in pubs, "drinking two bottles of whiskey a day," he said — but now he was "on the wagon" and walking miles each day to keep fit.

One wintry evening I picked him up at his caravan and we drove to Kilrush to discuss his scheme over dinner. All the time, I noticed, he kept the brief-case firmly between his feet. "It would be disastrous for me if it fell into the wrong hands," he said. "I carry it with me everywhere, even when on an eighteen-mile walk along the cliffs."

He then began to discuss his plan in low tones. "You know I engineered Blake's escape and got him to Moscow via East Berlin," he said. "He has lived over there ever since in the company of defectors like Kim Philby. For me it is very different. After years of living in isolation I've now decided to give myself up to the British to face trial, "I want to make a clean breast of the whole thing." Later Bourke mentioned a number of well-known people, including a British actress, and a wealthy woman heiress who provided money — to help the escape plans, he said. "The account of the Blake escape operation given in my book is substantially correct but certain names and addresses were changed," he added.

Bourke, who seemed to possess a photographic memory, also showed me copies of his original manuscripts done during his stay in Moscow with Blake and censored by KGB headquarters.

When I left him that night, back at Kilkee, he was still hugging his precious brief-case. As we had a last pint before he made his way back to his caravan he said, "I'll put my scheme in writing to your paper"* This is the letter he sent by registered post in September 1981 — a letter which will be of ongoing interest in view of the notorious Foreign Office spy case:

'You will be aware that the British Foreign Office man, George Blake, was sentenced in 1961 to forty-two years imprisonment for spying for the Soviet Union and that this sentence was the longest ever imposed in a British court of law. You will also be aware that in October 1966 George Blake escaped from Wormwood Scrubs Prison after he had served only five years of this forty-two-year sentence.

'It is now a matter of public record that it was this writer who engineered Blake's escape and spirited him to Moscow, via East Berlin, where Blake has lived in retirement ever since in the company of other defectors like Kim Philby.

'I myself followed Blake to Moscow where I spent two years writing a book about the venture. I returned to Ireland in October 1968 and shortly afterwards the British authorities sent a warrant to Dublin seeking my extradition. My case was heard first in the High Court where it was decided that I could not be extradited on the grounds that my offence was political. The British appealed this decision to the Supreme Court which upheld the decision of the High Court by the very generous majority of four to one. I was thus freed for

---

* *News of the World*, who have kindly given permission to publish.

all time from the possibility of being put on trial and imprisoned by the British courts for my offence.

'However, after years of living in this self-inflicted limbo I have now decided to give myself up to the British authorities to face trial and, inevitably, go to jail. This is why I am writing to you. I have a proposition to put to you which might be to our mutual benefit.

'I propose to cross the Northern Ireland Border and surrender myself to Special Branch officers from Scotland Yard, having first written to the Metropolitan Police Commissioner to inform him of my plans and to give him the exact date, time and place of the Border crossing. (There is a touch of irony there somewhere. My 'exile' from Britain began with my crossing one border at Checkpoint Charlie and is now to end with my crossing another border straight into the United Kingdom and the arms of the law.)

'Briefly, I am offering your newspaper exclusive coverage of this story in its every aspect. This would include exclusive photographs of the border crossing, the surrender to Scotland Yard officers, a detailed background story written by me, and of course an in-depth interview.

'I would make information available to you that has never before been revealed and that might well be regarded as sensational. This would include the name of the highly respectable organization without whose very active help Blake's escape could not have taken place. An organization whose leaders are to be found in the pages of *Who's Who*. And this is not just idle talk; I can provide the conclusive proof.

'Why am I doing this? I have suffered a great deal for springing George Blake from Wormwood Scrubs, more than anyone will ever know. And of course it serves me right. I walked into it with my eyes wide open. Now, however, I want to make a clean breast of the whole thing, stand my trial at the Old Bailey, serve my sentence, and then hopefully sink into oblivion as a purely private citizen at long last.

'From your point of view, this could prove to be one of the most dramatic stories you have ever published and it could quite easily be spread out over a period of four weeks. This is what I propose:

(1) I would write a detailed background story which would include certain aspects of the escape and its aftermath not hitherto made public. I would also deal in detail with any points which you considered should be elaborated upon.

(2) I would co-operate with your reporters in an in-depth interview or interviews 'with no holds barred'.

(3) I would name the organization without whose help and *active*

participation George Blake could not have escaped from Wormwood Scrubs. And I would produce conclusive proof.

(4) I would be available for any promotional material such as motion film or video advertising in connection with the series of articles.

(5) I would envisage crossing the Border on a Saturday afternoon with only *your* reporters and photographers in attendance. With your background material already prepared this would give your newspaper a front-page world exclusive the following morning. And of course you would have the ready-made advantage of ten years of unrelenting publicity that has surrounded the Irish border. Publicity that just could not be bought.

(6) The above in itself would be a very valuable exclusive story, but for your newspaper it would be only the beginning. There would be a very dramatic and highly-publicized trial at the Old Bailey generating a great deal of interest in Britain and Europe and in the United States. With the benefit of this highly valuable publicity, you would launch your exclusive series of articles, using also the promotional material already referred to above.

(7) Your newspaper could not lose in this transaction. The fee agreed on would be paid by cheque to my solicitor in Limerick *after* my trial at the Old Bailey. Furthermore, it could only be good for the image of your newspaper to have encouraged me to surrender and face trial.

'I can be contacted at the above address, where I shall be staying until I am ready to travel to the Border. I have in fact been using this caravan for the past few months and taking daily walks along the Atlantic coast to contemplate my future. I have now made a final decision, the most important decision of my life.'

Yours faithfully,
(SEAN BOURKE)

Some time later he changed his mind about his plan to give himself up at the Border but was still anxious to give the 'full, frank inside story of the Blake escape disclosing names of public figures involved for the first time'.

He explained: "I've been investigating and I find that living conditions in Britain's prisons now are quite frightening — three men locked into the space of a small bathroom, with three chamber-pots and virtually no ventilation for twenty hours a day. No, thank you. At Wormwood Scrubs I had my own cell, my own private office where I worked full time as editor of the prison magazine, complete with gas-ring, a television set, and a blue band on my arm enabling me to go anywhere I pleased, and to escort other prisoners. I had better working conditions than the screws!"

Sean probably made a wise decision — but there were still those secrets of his. And his constant fear of someone or some persons. (Those sensational disclosures of September 1981 were splashed — more than SIX YEARS later — in one of the Sunday heavies as a big Scoop!)

After the shock news of his death his brother Kevin, who lives in Scotland, told me: "I'm trying to clear up his estate. After the funeral I collected his few belongings from the hospital in Ennis. I also visited the caravan at Kilkee. The police had already removed his typewriter, radio and a few odds and ends of papers which did not amount to very much.

"So far I am unable to trace any manuscripts — in fact there are lots of things which I am unable to trace. I have also been told that he always carried a brief-case containing his more personal papers with him, even on his longer walks around the countryside near Kilkee. But needless to say, I am unable to trace the brief-case. I am particularly worried because I know that some of his 'friends' from Limerick visited the caravan on the same evening that he passed away."

Sean Bourke died on the morning of 26 January, 1982 just after starting out on one of his walks. Previously he had appeared to be in robust health. An inquest was told there was no sign of chronic alcoholism and the opinion was given that death was due to coronary thrombosis. But the enigma remains — Who was he afraid of? Was he attacked during that lonely cliff-side walk? Why did he carry a revolver for his own protection? Who took the brief-case containing his precious secrets?

Questions which still remain unanswered — but other problems affecting the future of all newspapermen were daily growing more serious. . .

Chapter 26

THE REVOLUTION

'It was like the Sinking of the Titanic'
It ain't no use to grumble and complain.
It's jest as cheap and easy to rejoice.
When He sorts out the weather and sends rain
Why, rain's my choice!   *—James Whitcomb Riley*

The famous Fleet Street that had been the heartland of national newspapers for centuries, the revered area that had been a constant magnet to ambitious pressmen, was — unbelievably — being crippled, broken up and decimated in the mid-1980s. The unthinkable happened and 'the Street' became a killing-ground not just through onslaughts from without but because of greed, weaknesses and strife from within.

For decades management failings and printing union disputes had beset the press. Unions took increasing advantage of the weaknesses. Sudden stoppages, often just before press time, were planned. In the editorial department we soon learned to read the signs. For example, when the lino and machine-men arrived without their lunch-boxes a stoppage was inevitable! Many managers, with indifferent training, had little idea of how to deal with aggressive union spokesmen. The more they wavered the greater the demands. This in turn led to costly abuses, hugely inflated shift payments, big wage packets to 'ghost workers'.

Old titles such as the *Daily Sketch*, *Empire News*, *Sunday Chronicle*, *News Chronicle* were early casualties not just of circulation battles but of ineffective management. The *Sunday Dispatch*, a leading paper, became the prize victim in the sixties when its able editor Charles Eade — who had built up circulation to over 2,500,000, then the second highest in Fleet Street — was not afforded full support at a critical period. This situation came to a head after a malicious speech by the egotistical Randolph Churchill in which he referred to the then Lord Rothermere, Chairman of Associated Newspapers, as 'the Pornographer-Royal of England'. It was, of course, a foolish unjustified charge and, coming from such an irresponsible source, should have been ignored.

But instead of laughing off the affair the management began interfering in the content of the paper, and ordered the scrapping of popular features including the Bathing Beauty Contest. Eade (and his loyal assistant Chris Petersen) resisted, tried to ride out the situation and save the paper — but as sales fell and his authority was undermined he resigned. Some of the editors who succeeded him were ineffective — one so much so that he took to lying behind a couch so that callers would think he was out of his office. The chaos and mismanagement on the paper at the time were pitiful to witness — lack of control, in-fighting among the 'top brass', cynicism all round. In this atmosphere on the 160-year-old paper standards fell to zero. I saw one top editorial executive grab the proofs from another and in the resultant row threaten to throw his rival out of the window.

This part of a letter written by a staffer to a colleague just before the close-down in 1961 illustrates the collapse of morale on the 'sinking ship': 'Things are disintegrating rapidly here now. As you may have heard A . . . has gone. B . . . goes in a week or two. C . . . is on the move. Most of the others are thoroughly fed up. The powers of the paper spend their afternoons at strip shows and lurch back at 5 p.m. Or else they come back from lunch at 3.30 and go out again at 4.30 for a drink. More often than not the set-up consists of a non-decision-making don't-want-to-be-involved D . . . and E . . . One fed-up reporter continually threatens to resign and spends many of his nights in a drunken stupor or at the Turkish baths.'

A comical incident relieved the gloom of this period. The Northern Editor Aubrey Viggars invited one new London editor to lunch at the Midland Hotel, Manchester, to meet the Northern staffs. The time was arranged — 12.30 for drinks before the meal.

Aubrey, who had been appointed by Charles Eade and was, like him, a stickler for efficiency and time-keeping, had booked a function room for the event and arranged the menu and wines. All was ready at the appointed hour, and hosts and hotel staff waited . . . and waited and waited . . . 12.30 . . . 1.30 . . . 2.30 . . . but no editor arrived. Then . . . a phone call. It was the editor calling from . . . Staffordshire! He had decided to travel by car and he and his driver had underestimated the distance. A disgusted Aubrey Viggars exclaimed, "Obviously hasn't a clue where Manchester is. Let's get on with our lunch."

The distinguished guest on his eventual arrival had to make do with a cold plate — and a somewhat ironical reception.

*   *   *

The *News of the World* was at the centre of the revolution in the mid-1980s that resulted in the demise of Fleet Street, and also the reduction of Manchester as the great newspaper production centre in the north of England. The printing unions had for years resisted the introduction of new technology, and it was first Eddie Shah and then Rupert Murdoch, the Australian tycoon, who managed to smash their opposition.

* *

"Rupert Murdoch's not an armchair newspaper tycoon.
He can take a front page apart and re-jig it on the deadline"
— A journalist at Wapping.

* *

On taking over the *News of the World* one of the first things Murdoch did was to send for Stafford Somerfield, who had been a popular editor for ten years and who during the ownership struggle had hit out against the 'predators', declaring in a leader 'The *News of the World* is as British as roast beef and Yorkshire pudding'. (Under his editorship it was in fact a comparatively good newspaper then with good law court reporting, features and news coverage — saucy of course, but not the type of tabloid to which it was later reduced.)

In short, Somerfield was asked for his resignation despite his successful record as editor. Most of the staff greatly resented his dismissal. There was talk of a protest strike, but many members were concerned about their own jobs at the time and nothing was done. After Somerfield's departure there was a succession of editors. Some of the appointments were astonishing and four of these lasted only for brief periods.

Then came the 'revolution' in Fleet Street and Murdoch's amazing coup that defeated the print unions. While the war against and within the unions was going on Murdoch and his aides were secretly perfecting the great new plant at Wapping behind high metal fencing, with its advanced computer systems and latest techniques. Also in secret, coachloads of technicians were being driven in daily for training in the new technology.

Then the crunch came, the strikes started, violence spread. But Murdoch persisted, carried on the battle started by Eddie Shah — and won. In the process he sacked thousands of print men who thought they had an eternal stranglehold on Fleet Street — and Manchester. Union spokesmen accused him of 'bullying and oppression from behind coils of razor wire'. Murdoch retorted, "The print unions have been bullies for years. They are impossible to deal with. There's only one thing they understand."

The periods before and after January 1986 when Rupert Murdoch's 'journos' in Bouverie Street eventually agreed to move to Wapping were marked by the longest and worst confrontations and violence ever experienced in the newspaper industry. During the years before the Wapping coup — when the print unions had the power and some operatives had bargained themselves up to over £800 a week — furious disputes and stoppages recurred, usually around midnight.

Then the phone in one's home would ring. The news-desk — "No paper being printed tonight. There's been another stoppage. Another row in the black hole. Too bad about your story." Too bad indeed, especially if the story, as occurred on occasion, was to be the 'splash'.

The 'black hole', a deafening whirl of metal, newsprint and ink spray, was the notorious machine-room in Bouverie Street (Fleet Street) which poured out papers in their millions. With its old and overloaded presses and arduous working conditions this place became a metaphorical battleground of the time. The machine-room crews were hard men but with fierce loyalty — one stoppage which lasted four days was sparked off by just one word, the word 'scum' in a story referring not to themselves but to certain miners.

There were lurid stories then of angry confrontations involving such personages as Ray James, the Father of the Sogat machine-room chapel, an outspoken boss with great power among the men; Kelvin MacKenzie, the controversial and even more abrasive Editor of the *Sun*; Bruce Matthews, managing director of News International; John Breen, deputy Imperial Father of the *News of the World* composing room; Ernie Hardcastle, Ray James's deputy; John Brown of the NGA, Tony Isaacs of Sogat, both Imperial Fathers of their chapels, and others.

The disputes along with rows about overtime claims caused trains to be missed and big losses in circulation. During one row machine-room men tore away the paper and pulled the plates from the presses to end the print runs.

But while all this strife was going on Rupert Murdoch and his planners were busily mocking-up the Atex computer system. This was an amazing operation carried out in secret in a warehouse, code-named The Bunker, at Woolwich — the preliminary to Wapping. Such was the hush-hush atmosphere then that the American experts who installed the system lived at clandestine addresses.

With the revolution out went the centuries-old hot-metal method of linotype newspaper composition, and in came the new 'direct input' computer techniques. In the maze of new equipment some seasoned reporters like Peter Earle and Ron Mount could be heard to murmur, "Anybody got a decent old-fashioned typewriter?"

Murdoch won all right, but after the 'revolution' a lot of things were never the same again. Including journalistic standards. Many long-standing friendships among journalists themselves were shattered. They broke up in recriminations and jealousies over redundancies, dismissals, transfers and new appointments.

In those bitter days it was impossible, staffers found, to contact some long-time 'friends' and supposed colleagues even by telephone. "It's like the sinking of the Titanic. It's every man for himself now," said one newsman bitterly.

The personal dramas resulted in some broken homes as well as broken friendships.

But Rupert Murdoch commented afterwards in reply to accusations of ruthlessness, "A revolution had to come. Fleet Street and Manchester were hopelessly out of date. Those fellows in the print unions gave me seventeen years of hell. I brought order and efficiency into the newspaper industry. It was bloody exciting while it lasted!"

It's been said of Murdoch that he loves newspapers but hasn't much time for journalists, that he's become a 'sinister force' because of all his world-wide newspaper and television interests. He certainly can have had no feelings of respect or sentiment for the rich history and background of Fleet Street which over the centuries has been trod by a host of famous personalities. One of the first great journalists, Daniel Defoe — the subsequent author of *Robinson Crusoe* — was placed in the pillory at Newgate in the year 1703 after writing a tract on behalf of religious toleration. One isn't suggesting that someone today should be similarly dealt with, but Fleet Street — where Addison, Pope, Steele, Johnson, Goldsmith, Boswell, Dickens and so many other renowned literary men flourished — remains in its way hallowed ground. Dr Johnson loved to stroll along it towards the Cheshire Cheese, touching the posts as he passed and remarking to Boswell, "How cheerful and animated the Street looks this morning." Sentimental, perhaps. Galsworthy wrote: 'The price of sentiment is the amount of sacrifice you are prepared to make for it.' There wasn't any sentiment during the Fleet Street 'revolution' and, when it came to the 'numbers game', history and tradition never even entered the computerized mentalities.

A long-time colleague stunned by events at the time exclaimed, "The end of Fleet Street — I can't believe it! Is nothing sacred?"

Like myself he had started out on a country weekly paper and he, too, had spent years in Fleet Street and now shared the frustration of many journalists, uncertain of their future and disgusted with the cynical turn of events.

Then he said, "I think I'll pack it in, collect what redundancy money I can get, and find a job on a provincial paper. After all, I began on one."

Brightening up, he went on, "Let's look at the situation this way. I've been lucky. We've been lucky. We've had some great times, got some very good stories — and had a lot of laughs into the bargain doing the work we like best — on newspapers. When you think of it, who could ask for anything more?"

"True — quite right," I agreed. "Dear old Fleet Street — gone as we knew it but not forgotten. Goodbye to the one-time Street of Adventure. We've had those good times and, as a bonus — what luck! — all those laughs. . . ." (We went free-lancing.)

And finally, talking of laughs, these lines by the observant Gwendolen Haste are appropriate:

I had to laugh
For when she said it we were sitting by the door
And straight down was The Fork
Twisting and turning and gleaming in the sun.
And then your eyes carried across the purple beach beyond the river
With the Beartooth Mountains fairly screaming with light and blue and snow
And fold and turn of rimrock and prairie, as far as your eye could go.
And she says, "Dear Laura, sometimes I feel so sorry for you
Shut away from everything — eating your heart out with loneliness.
When I think of my own full life I wish that I could share it.
Just pray for happier days to come, and bear it."
She goes back to Billings — to her white stucco house
And looks through net curtains at another white stucco house
And a brick house
And a yellow frame house
And six trimmed poplar trees
And little squares of shaved grass.
Oh, dear — she stared at me like I was daft.
I couldn't help it! I just laughed and laughed.

INDEX